KT-495-929

MURDOCH BOOKS

Published by Murdoch Books Pty Limited.

Murdoch Books Australia
Pier 8/9, 23 Hickson Road
Millers Point NSW 2000
Phone: + 61 (0)2 8220 2000
Fax: + 61 (0)2 8220 2558

Murdoch Books UK Limited
Erico House, 6th Floor North
93–99 Upper Richmond Road
Putney, London SW15 2TG
Phone: + 44 (0) 20 8785 5995
Fax: + 44 (0) 20 8785 5985

Chief Executive: Juliet Rogers
Publisher: Kay Scarlett

Design Manager: Vivien Valk
Design Concept, Design and Illustration: Alex Frampton
Project Manager and editor: Jacqueline Blanchard
Introduction text: Leanne Kitchen
Recipes developed by the Murdoch Books Test Kitchen
Production: Monika Paratore

National Library of Australia Cataloguing-in-Publication Data:
Plum, pudding, pie : a cook's book of Christmas.
Includes index. ISBN 1 74045 740 4.
1. Christmas cookery. 641.5686

Printed by Midas Printing (Asia) Ltd. in 2005. PRINTED IN CHINA.

IMPORTANT: Those who might be at risk from the effects of salmonella poisoning (the elderly, pregnant women, young children and those suffering from immune deficiency diseases) should consult their doctor with any concerns about eating raw eggs.

CONVERSION GUIDE: You may find cooking times vary depending on the oven you are using. For fan-forced ovens, as a general rule, set the oven temperature to 20°C (35°F) lower than indicated in the recipe. We have used 20 ml (4 teaspoon) tablespoon measures. If you are using a 15 ml (3 teaspoon) tablespoon, for most recipes the difference will not be noticeable. However, for recipes using baking powder, gelatine, bicarbonate of soda (baking soda), small amounts of flour and cornflour (cornstarch), add an extra teaspoon for each tablespoon specified.

a cook's book of christmas
PLUM
PUDDING
PIE

Contents

A very merry Christmas

Thank goodness for Christmas! No matter where in the world we might be, this is always a magical time, marked by long holidays, generous giving, charming rituals and luxurious, unrestrained feasting. Tables groan with glossy, glazed hams, steaming dishes of vegetables, icy bowls of zesty punch, and myriad other accompaniments. Platters that heave with juicy roasts of turkey, duck or pork; decadent, boozy trifle; and sweet favourites such as tender, buttery shortbread — all spark cherished memories that link us to our childhoods, our forebears, and generations of celebrators the globe over.

With their origins obscured deep in centuries past, many of the traditional dishes we so enjoy at this time of year are not just delicious, but have profound historical significance as well, some even predating Christmas itself. The beloved plum pudding tradition is said to have begun with the Druids when dense, fruit-filled sweets were made to celebrate the winter solstice. Marzipan came to Europe from the Middle East with the Crusaders, and has somehow become a Christmas staple in many cultures. Mincemeat tarts date from medieval England, when it was perfectly customary to simmer ground beef, sweet spices, sugar, dried fruits and alcohol together until it formed a sticky, lush pie filling. Families may develop their own unique customs and preferred menus for Christmas, but universally loved and anticipated for weeks before are the seductive aromas of crisping meats, fruity cakes, traditional breads and brandied sauces and drinks.

The flavours of Christmas are unmistakable. Vanilla, cinnamon, cloves and nutmeg are the soul-warming spices of Christmas while savoury fare is spiked with aromatic hints of sage, citrus and rosemary. Chestnuts, cranberries, horseradish and jewel-like glacé fruits pervading stuffings, sauces and side-dishes also form the basis of after-dinner treats. Nuts in their shells, blue cheese and port and wickedly potent eggnog are other singular treats that signal the Christmas season. Opulence is the cornerstone of festive entertaining: champagne, oysters, tender birds, top-quality chocolate, and the season's prime fruits and vegetables are appropriate for voluptuous Christmas spreads. All the trimmings and finishing touches are equally expressive of the yuletide spirit too, with perfect, glowing candles, crisp napery, sparkling silverware, hand-formed rum truffles and sprigs of bright greenery as crucial as the menu in creating unforgettable Christmas days.

Eggnog Custard Roast Turkey Pudding Fru

Starters

Spicy Nuts

Serves 6

2 tablespoons olive oil
$\frac{1}{2}$ teaspoon ground cumin
$\frac{1}{2}$ teaspoon ground coriander leaves
$\frac{1}{2}$ teaspoon garlic powder
$\frac{1}{4}$ teaspoon chilli powder
$\frac{1}{4}$ teaspoon ground ginger
$\frac{1}{4}$ teaspoon ground cinnamon
65 g ($2\frac{1}{4}$ oz/$\frac{2}{3}$ cup) pecans
100 g ($3\frac{1}{2}$ oz/$\frac{2}{3}$ cup) raw cashew nuts
240 g ($8\frac{1}{2}$ oz/$1\frac{1}{2}$ cups) raw almonds

1 Preheat the oven to 150°C (300°F/Gas 2). Heat the oil over low heat in a pan and stir in the spices for 2 minutes, or until fragrant. Remove from the heat, add the nuts and stir with a wooden spoon until the nuts are well coated. Spread over a baking tray and bake for 15 minutes, or until golden. Sprinkle with salt and cool.

Smoked Salmon Tartlets

Makes 24

250 g (9 oz/1 cup) cream cheese, at room temperature
1 1/2 tablespoons wholegrain mustard
2 teaspoons dijon mustard
2 tablespoons lemon juice
2 tablespoons chopped dill
6 sheets frozen puff pastry, thawed
300 g (10 1/2 oz) smoked salmon, cut into strips
2 tablespoons capers, rinsed and squeezed dry
fresh dill sprigs, to garnish

1. Preheat the oven to 210°C (415°F/Gas 6–7). Line two large baking trays with baking paper. Mix the cream cheese, mustards, lemon juice and dill in a bowl, then cover and refrigerate.
2. Cut four 9.5 cm (3 3/4 inch) rounds from each sheet of puff pastry, using a fluted cutter, and place on the baking trays. Prick the pastries all over. Cover and refrigerate for 10 minutes.
3. Bake the pastries in batches for 7 minutes, then remove from the oven and use a spoon to flatten the centre of each pastry. Return to the oven and bake for another 5 minutes, or until the pastry is golden. Cool, then spread some of the cream cheese mixture over each pastry, leaving a 1 cm (1/2 inch) border. Arrange the salmon over the top. Decorate with a few capers and a sprig of fresh dill. Serve immediately.

Oysters with Bloody Mary Sauce

Makes 24

24 oysters, on the half-shell
60 ml (2 fl oz/1/4 cup) tomato juice
2 teaspoons vodka
1 teaspoon lemon juice
1/2 teaspoon worcestershire sauce
dash of Tabasco sauce
1 celery stalk
chives, snipped, to garnish

1. Remove 24 oysters from their shells. Clean and dry the shells.
2. Combine the tomato juice, vodka, lemon juice, worcestershire sauce and a few drops of Tabasco sauce in a small bowl. Cut the celery stalk into very thin strips and place in the bases of the oyster shells. Top with an oyster and drizzle with tomato mixture. Sprinkle with 1–2 teaspoons of chives.

Watercress Soup

Serves 8

1 large onion, chopped
4 spring onions (scallions), chopped
450 g (1 lb) watercress, chopped
115 g (4 oz) butter
40 g (1½ oz/⅓ cup) plain (all-purpose) flour
600 ml (21 fl oz/2⅓ cups) ready-made chicken stock
500 ml (17 fl oz/2 cups) water
sour cream and sprigs of watercress, to garnish

1. Melt the butter in a large heavy-based saucepan. Add the onion, spring onions and watercress and cook over a low heat, stirring for 3 minutes, or until the vegetables have softened. Stir in the flour.
2. Mix together the stock and water and gradually add to the pan, stirring until the mixture is smooth. Stir constantly over a medium heat for 10 minutes, or until the mixture boils and thickens. Boil for 1 minute further. Remove from the heat and set aside to cool.
3. In batches, put the cooled mixture in a blender or food processor. Blend for 15 seconds, or until the mixture is smooth. Return the soup to the saucepan and gently heat through. Serve warm, garnished with sour cream and watercress sprigs.

Blue Cheese and Port Pâté

Serves 8

350 g (12 oz/$1\frac{1}{3}$ cups) cream cheese, at room temperature
60 g ($2\frac{1}{4}$ oz) unsalted butter, softened
80 ml ($2\frac{1}{2}$ fl oz/$\frac{1}{3}$ cup) port
300 g ($10\frac{1}{2}$ oz) blue cheese, at room temperature, mashed
1 tablespoon snipped fresh chives
50 g ($1\frac{3}{4}$ oz/$\frac{1}{2}$ cup) walnut halves

1. Beat the cream cheese and butter in a small bowl until smooth, then stir in the port. Add the blue cheese and chives and stir until just combined. Season, to taste. Spoon into a serving dish and smooth the surface. Cover with plastic wrap and refrigerate for 3–4 hours, or until firm.

2. Arrange the walnuts over the top and press in lightly. Serve at room temperature. Makes a delicious spread on crusty bread, crackers, celery stalks or wedges of firm fruit, such as apple and pear.

Corn and Potato Fritters

Makes about 40

2 large potatoes

265 g ($9^{1}/_{2}$ oz/$1^{1}/_{3}$ cups) tinned corn kernels, drained

4 eggs, lightly beaten

6 spring onions (scallions), chopped

50 g ($1^{3}/_{4}$ oz/$^{1}/_{2}$ cup) dry breadcrumbs

1 teaspoon garam masala

3 tablespoons oil

DIPPING SAUCE

160 g ($5^{3}/_{4}$ oz/$^{2}/_{3}$ cup) plain yoghurt

2 tablespoons chopped mint

2 teaspoons sweet chilli sauce

1. Peel and coarsely grate the potatoes. Drain on paper towels and squeeze out the excess moisture. Combine in a bowl with the corn, eggs, spring onion, breadcrumbs and garam masala. Mix well.
2. To make the dipping sauce, combine all the ingredients in a bowl.
3. Heat 2 tablespoons of the oil in a heavy-based frying pan over medium heat. Cook heaped tablespoons of the mixture for 2 minutes on each side, or until golden. Drain on crumpled paper towels and keep warm. Repeat until all the mixture is used, adding extra oil to the frying pan if necessary. Serve with the dipping sauce.

Mini Lamb Pies

Makes about 12

FILLING
2 tablespoons olive oil
1 onion, thinly sliced
2 garlic cloves, crushed
2 teaspoons ground cumin
2 teaspoons ground ginger
2 teaspoons paprika
1 teaspoon ground turmeric
1 teaspoon ground cinnamon
500 g (1 lb 2 oz) lamb fillet, diced
375 ml (13 fl oz/$1\frac{1}{2}$ cups) ready-made beef stock
1 tablespoon finely chopped preserved lemon peel
2 tablespoons pitted kalamata olives, sliced
1 tablespoon chopped coriander (cilantro) leaves

750 g (1 lb 10 oz) ready-rolled shortcrust pastry
1 egg, lightly beaten

1. To make the filling, heat the oil in a large saucepan over medium heat, then add the onion, garlic and spices. Coat the lamb in the spice mixture, then pour in the stock. Cover and cook over low heat for 30 minutes. Add the preserved lemon and cook, uncovered, for a further 20 minutes, or until the liquid has reduced and the lamb is tender. Stir in the olives and coriander, then leave to cool.
2. Preheat the oven to 180°C (350°F/Gas 4) and put a baking tray in the oven. Grease twelve 5 cm (2 inch) shallow tart moulds.

3 Roll the pastry thinly and cut out 12 rounds with an 8 cm (3 1/4 inch) cutter. Then, using a 5.5 cm (2 1/4 inch) cutter, cut out 12 smaller rounds from the remaining pastry. Put one of the larger rounds in each tart mould and fill with the cooled filling. Dampen the edges of the small rounds and put them on top of the filling to seal the pies. Trim the edges and brush with egg. Put the tart moulds on the hot baking tray and bake for 20 minutes, or until golden. Cool slightly, then remove the pies from the moulds. Serve immediately.

Herbed Chicken Drumsticks

Makes 12

12 small chicken drumsticks
115 g (4 oz) butter
1 onion, grated
1/2 teaspoon grated lemon zest
2 tablespoons finely chopped parsley
1 tablespoon finely chopped mint
1 tablespoon finely chopped coriander (cilantro) leaves
1/2 teaspoon chilli sauce
1 tablespoon lemon juice
1 tablespoon honey
2 teaspoons soy sauce

1. Preheat the oven to 180°C (350°F/Gas 4). Wash the drumsticks and pat them dry with paper towels. Loosen the skin around each drumstick with your finger to form a pocket for the herb mixture.
2. Beat together the butter, onion and lemon zest until just combined. Add the herbs and chilli sauce and stir until just combined.
3. Divide the mixture into 12 portions. Place one portion of herb mixture under the skin of each drumstick. Hold the skin over the filling, and press gently to distribute the herb mixture.
4. Arrange the drumsticks in a single layer over the base of a shallow baking dish. Combine the lemon juice, honey and soy sauce in a small bowl. Brush the mixture over the drumsticks. Bake for 20 minutes, basting occasionally with the lemon mixture. Turn the drumsticks over, baste again and bake for a further 25 minutes. Serve warm or cold, garnished with parsley.

Baby Caviar Potatoes

Makes 30

30 baby new potatoes (choose very small potatoes of a similar size)
250 g (9 oz/1 cup) sour cream
2 tablespoons caviar (red or black, or both)

1. Preheat the oven to 200°C (400°F/Gas 6). Prick the potatoes with a fork and put them on a baking tray. Bake for 40 minutes, or until tender. Cool to room temperature.
2. Cut a large cross in the top of each potato and squeeze open. Top with a small dollop of sour cream and a little caviar.

Chicken Liver and Grand Marnier Pâté

Serves 8

750 g (1 lb 10 oz) chicken livers, well trimmed
250 ml (9 fl oz/1 cup) milk
200 g (7 oz) butter, softened
4 spring onions (scallions), finely chopped
1 tablespoon Grand Marnier
1 tablespoon orange juice concentrate
1/2 orange, very thinly sliced

JELLY LAYER
1 tablespoon orange juice concentrate
1 tablespoon Grand Marnier
315 ml (10 3/4 fl oz/1 1/4 cups) tinned chicken consommé, undiluted
2 1/2 teaspoons powdered gelatine

1. Put the chicken livers in a bowl, add the milk and stir to combine. Cover and refrigerate for 1 hour. Drain the livers and discard the milk. Rinse in cold water, drain and pat dry with paper towels.
2. Melt a third of the butter in a frying pan, add the spring onions and cook for 2–3 minutes, or until tender, but not brown. Add the livers and cook, stirring, over medium heat for 4–5 minutes, or until just cooked. Remove from the heat and cool a little.
3. Transfer the livers and spring onions to a food processor and process until very smooth. Chop the remaining butter and add to the mixture with the Grand Marnier and orange juice concentrate. Continue to blend until creamy. Season with salt and freshly ground black pepper, to taste. Transfer to a 1.25 litre (44 fl oz) serving dish, cover the surface with plastic wrap and chill for 1 1/2 hours, or until firm.

4. To make the jelly layer, whisk together the orange juice concentrate, Grand Marnier and 125 ml (4 fl oz/1/2 cup) of the consommé in a jug. Sprinkle the gelatine over the liquid in an even layer and leave until the gelatine is spongy—do not stir. Heat the remaining consommé in a saucepan, remove from the heat and add the gelatine mixture. Stir to dissolve the gelatine, then leave to cool and thicken to the consistency of uncooked egg white, but not set.
5. Press the orange slices lightly into the surface of the pâté and spoon the thickened jelly evenly over the top. Refrigerate until set.

Pâté can be made a couple of days ahead and is best served at room temperature with savoury crackers or bread. Grand Marnier is a cognac-based liqueur with an orange flavour.

Chicken and Tarragon Vol au Vents

Makes 12

1 small chicken breast fillet
250 ml (9 fl oz/1 cup) cream (whipping)
1 tablespoon finely chopped tarragon
1 spring onion (scallion), finely chopped
12 mini vol au vent pastry shells

1. Preheat the oven to 170°C (325°F/Gas 3). Put the chicken fillet in a small saucepan of salted boiling water. Cover, turn off the heat and poach the chicken for about 20 minutes. Remove and cool before cutting the chicken into very small cubes.
2. Put the cream in a small saucepan and bring to boiling point. Reduce the heat and simmer for 5–10 minutes, or until the cream is very thick. Stir in the chicken, tarragon and spring onion. While still warm, spoon the filling into the pastry shells, piling the filling up. Bake for 8 minutes. Serve hot.

Fruity Meatballs

Makes about 64

500 g (1 lb 2 oz) minced (ground) beef
1 onion, grated
4 tablespoons fruit chutney (see page 137)
1 tablespoon worcestershire sauce
8 tablespoons dried breadcrumbs
1 egg, lightly beaten
1/2 teaspoon garlic salt
1/4 teaspoon pepper
120 ml (4 fl oz/1/2 cup) vegetable oil
1 tablespoon chopped parsley

1. Put the beef, onion, chutney, worcestershire sauce, breadcrumbs, egg, garlic salt and pepper in a bowl and mix until thoroughly combined. Taking 2 teaspoons of the mixture at a time, form it into balls by rolling between the palms of your hands.

2. Heat the oil in a heavy-based frying pan. Add the meatballs and cook, in batches, over a medium heat for 5 minutes, or until golden brown and cooked through. Remove from the pan with a slotted spoon and drain on paper towels. If serving the meatballs hot, keep warm while you cook the remaining meatballs. Transfer the meatballs to a serving dish, garnish with parsley and serve hot or cold with your favourite dipping sauce.

Grilled Mussels

Serves 2–4

500 g fresh mussels, scrubbed and beards removed
2 tablespoons lemon juice
1 garlic clove, crushed
1 small red chilli, seeded and finely chopped
3 teaspoons finely chopped parsley

1. Put the mussels in a pan of simmering water. Remove the mussels as the shells open. Discard any mussels that do not open after 5 minutes.
2. Open the mussels and loosen from the shells using scissors. Return them to half shells and discard the empty halves.
3. Mix together the lemon juice, garlic and chilli in a small bowl and spoon the mixture over the mussels. Place the mussels in a single layer on a grill rack or baking tray and cook under a preheated medium grill (broiler) until heated through. Sprinkle the mussels with the parsley and serve immediately.

Cheese Fruit Log

Serves 6

35 g (1¼ oz/¼ cup) shelled pistachio nuts
250 g (9 oz/1 cup) cream cheese, at room temperature
50 g (1¾ oz/¼ cup) dried apricots, finely chopped
3 spring onions (scallions), finely chopped
45 g (1½ oz/¼ cup) sun-dried tomatoes, finely chopped
3 tablespoons finely chopped flat-leaf (Italian) parsley

1. Preheat the oven to 200°C (400°F/Gas 6). Bake the pistachio nuts on a lined baking tray for 5 minutes, or until golden brown. Cool, then finely chop.
2. Beat the cream cheese in a bowl until smooth. Fold in the dried apricots, spring onions, sun-dried tomatoes and some pepper, to taste.
3. Sprinkle the chopped pistachio nuts and parsley over a sheet of baking paper, shaping into a 20 x 6 cm (8 x 2½ inch) rectangle. Form the cream cheese mixture into a 20 cm (8 inch) log and roll in the nut mixture. Wrap in plastic wrap and refrigerate for 2–3 hours, or until firm. Serve with plain savoury biscuits.

Lemon Prawn Pâté

Serves 8

750 g (1 lb 10 oz) raw prawns (shrimp)
100 g (3 1/2 oz) butter
3 garlic cloves, crushed
1 teaspoon grated lemon zest
3 tablespoons lemon juice
1/4 teaspoon freshly grated nutmeg
2 tablespoons whole-egg mayonnaise
2 tablespoons snipped chives

1. Peel the prawns and gently pull out the dark vein from each prawn back, starting at the head end. Take off the tails.
2. Melt the butter in a frying pan. When it sizzles, add the garlic and prawns and stir for 3–4 minutes, or until the prawns are pink and cooked through. Allow to cool.
3. Transfer to a food processor, add the lemon zest, lemon juice and nutmeg and process for 20 seconds, or until roughly puréed. Season, to taste, add the mayonnaise and chives, then process for 20 seconds, or until combined. Spoon into a dish and chill for at least 1 hour, or until firm.
4. Remove from the refrigerator about 15 minutes before serving to soften the pâté slightly. Serve with slices of crusty bread.

Mini Eggs Florentine

Makes 24

8 slices white bread
1–2 tablespoons olive oil
12 quail eggs
2 teaspoons lemon juice
85 g (3 oz) butter, melted, cooled
2 teaspoons finely chopped basil
20 g (3/4 oz) butter, extra
50 g (1 3/4 oz) baby English spinach leaves

1. Preheat the oven to 180°C (350°F/Gas 4). Cut 24 rounds from the bread with a 4 cm (1 1/2 inch) cutter. Brush both sides of the rounds with the oil and bake for 10–15 minutes, or until golden brown.
2. Add the quail eggs to a saucepan of cold water, bring to the boil, stirring gently (to centre the yolks) and simmer for 4 minutes. Drain, then soak in cold water until cool.
3. Peel the eggs, then cut in half, remove the yolks and reserve the whites.
4. Purée the egg yolks and lemon juice together in a food processor for 10 seconds, or until smooth. Add the cooled melted butter in a thin stream. Add the chopped basil and mix until all ingredients are well combined.
5. Melt the extra butter in a pan, add the spinach leaves and toss until just wilted. Place a little on each bread round, top each with half an egg white and fill the cavity with the basil mixture.

Olive and Rosemary Palmiers

Makes 30

50 g ($1^3/4$ oz/$^1/3$ cup) chopped, pitted black olives
25 g (1 oz/$^1/4$ cup) grated parmesan cheese
1 tablespoon chopped rosemary
4 salami slices, chopped
2 tablespoons vegetable oil
2 teaspoons dijon mustard
2 sheets frozen puff pastry, thawed
olives and sprigs of rosemary to garnish

1. Preheat the oven to 200°C (400°F/Gas 6). Grease two baking trays. Blend the olives, cheese, rosemary, salami, oil and mustard in a food processor until mixture forms a paste.
2. Place a sheet of pastry on a work surface and spread evenly with half the olive paste. Fold two opposite sides over to meet, edge to edge in the centre. Fold once again, then fold the pastry over itself once more to give 8 layers of pastry.
3. Cut the folded pastry at 1 cm ($^1/2$ inch) intervals and place each palmier, cut-side-up, onto the prepared trays, allowing for spreading. Open the palmiers out slightly at the folded end to create a V shape. Repeat with the remaining pastry and olive paste. Bake for 15 minutes or until golden brown. Serve garnished with olives and rosemary sprigs.

Crab Cakes with Avocado Dip

Makes about 30

500 g (1 lb 2 oz/2 1/2 cups) frozen crab meat, thawed
115 g (4 oz/1 1/2 cups) fresh breadcrumbs
120 ml (4 fl oz/1/2 cup) whole-egg mayonnaise
4 spring onions (scallions), chopped
4 tablespoons chopped coriander (cilantro) leaves
2 tablespoons lemon juice
1 teaspoon grated lemon zest
1 teaspoon sambal oelek
2 eggs, lightly beaten
oil, for pan-frying

AVOCADO DIP
1 small ripe avocado
1 garlic clove, crushed
90 g (3 1/4 oz/1/3 cup) plain yoghurt
80 ml (2 1/2 fl oz/1/3 cup) water

1. Preheat the oven to 180°C (350°F/Gas 4). Combine the crab meat, breadcrumbs, mayonnaise, spring onions, coriander, lemon juice, lemon zest, sambal oelek and eggs in a large bowl.
2. Heat 1 tablespoon of the oil in a frying pan. Drop spoonfuls of the mixture, about 2 1/2 cm (1 inch) apart, into the pan. Cook over medium heat for 2 minutes, or until the undersides are golden. Turn and cook for 2 minutes more. Remove, drain on paper towels and keep warm. Repeat with the remaining mixture, adding more oil as needed.
3. To make the dip, blend the avocado, garlic, yoghurt and water in a bowl until smooth and creamy. Serve with the hot crab cakes.

Pork and Veal Terrine

Serves 6

8–10 thin bacon slices
1 tablespoon olive oil
1 onion, chopped
2 garlic cloves, crushed
1 kg (2 lb 4 oz) pork and veal mince
80 g (2¾ oz/1 cup) fresh breadcrumbs
1 egg, beaten
60 ml (2 fl oz/¼ cup) brandy
3 teaspoons chopped thyme
3 tablespoons chopped parsley

1. Preheat the oven to 180°C (350°F/Gas 4). Lightly grease a 25 x 11 cm (10 x 4¼ inch) terrine tin. Line the tin with the bacon so that it overlaps slightly and hangs over the sides.
2. Heat the oil in a frying pan, add the onion and garlic and cook for 2–3 minutes, or until the onion is soft. Cool, then mix with the mince, breadcrumbs, egg, brandy, thyme and parsley in a large bowl. Season with salt and pepper. Fry a small piece of the mixture to check the seasoning, and adjust if necessary.
3. Spoon the mixture into the bacon-lined terrine, pressing down firmly to avoid any air bubbles. Fold the bacon over the top of the terrine. Cover the tin with lightly greased foil and put the tin in a baking dish.

4 Pour enough boiling water in the baking dish to come halfway up the side of the terrine tin. Bake for 1–1 1/4 hours, or until the juices run clear when the terrine is pierced with a skewer. Remove the terrine from the water-filled baking dish and pour off the excess juices. Cover with foil, then put a piece of heavy cardboard, cut to fit, on top of the terrine. Put weights or food tins on top of the cardboard to compress the terrine. Refrigerate overnight, then cut into slices to serve.

The terrine can be made ahead of time and stored, covered, in the refrigerator for up to 5 days. It is suitable for serving as a light meal with salad or as part of a buffet.

Caraway Pikelets with Smoked Trout

Makes 30

50 g (1 3/4 oz/1/3 cup) wholemeal (whole-wheat) self-raising flour
1/2 teaspoon caraway seeds
40 g (1 1/2 oz) butter
1 egg, lightly beaten
120 ml (4 fl oz/1/2 cup) milk
2 tablespoons cream cheese, softened
115 g (5 1/2 oz) smoked trout, sliced
sprigs of marjoram, dill or parsley and lemon wedges, to garnish

1. To make the pikelets, sift the flour into a bowl and add the caraway seeds, making a well in the centre. Melt 15 g (1/2 oz) of the butter and whisk with the egg and milk. Add to the dry ingredients. Using a wooden spoon, stir until well combined, but do not overbeat.
2. Grease a large heavy-based frying pan with a little of the remaining butter. Allow 1 teaspoon of mixture for each pikelet, cooking four or five at a time. Cook until bubbles appear on the surface, then turn to brown the other side. Cool on a wire rack. Repeat until all the mixture is used.
3. To assemble, spread a little cream cheese on each pikelet and top with a piece of smoked trout. Make piles of four or five on a serving dish. Garnish with a sprig of marjoram, dill or parsley and a lemon wedge. Serve at room temperature.

Cucumber Rounds with Avocado and Turkey

Makes 30

3 Lebanese (short) cucumbers
100 g ($3^{1}/_{2}$ oz) smoked turkey, sliced
$^{1}/_{2}$ ripe avocado, mashed
1 garlic clove, crushed
2 tablespoons cranberry sauce
2 tablespoons sour cream
cranberry sauce, extra, to garnish
alfalfa sprouts or mustard cress, to garnish

1. Slice the cucumbers into 1.5 cm ($^{5}/_{8}$ inch) rounds to make 30 pieces. Cut 30 rounds from the turkey using a 3 cm ($1^{1}/_{4}$ inch) cutter.
2. Combine the avocado with the garlic, cranberry sauce and sour cream. Spoon 1 teaspoon onto each cucumber round and top with a round of turkey. Spoon a little cranberry sauce on the top and garnish with alfalfa sprouts.

Prawn Cocktails

Serves 4

60 g (2¹/4 oz/¹/4 cup) whole-egg mayonnaise
2 teaspoons tomato sauce
dash of Tabasco sauce
¹/4 teaspoon worcestershire sauce
2 teaspoons thick (double) cream
¹/4 teaspoon lemon juice
24 large prawns (shrimp), cooked, cooled
4 lettuce leaves, shredded
lemon wedges, for serving

1. Mix the mayonnaise, sauces, cream and lemon juice together in a small bowl.
2. Peel the cooked prawns and gently pull out the dark vein from each prawn back. Remove the heads and tails, leaving the tails intact on eight of them.
3. Divide the lettuce between four cocktail glasses. Arrange the prawns without tails in the glasses and drizzle with the sauce. Hang two of the remaining prawns with tails intact over the edge of each glass and serve with lemon wedges.

Puff Pastry Twists

Makes 96

2 sheets frozen puff pastry, thawed

1 egg, lightly beaten

80 g (2 3/4 oz/1/2 cup) sesame seeds, poppy seeds or caraway seeds

1. Preheat the oven to 200°C (400°F/Gas 6). Lightly grease two baking trays. Brush the pastry with the egg and sprinkle with the sesame seeds.
2. Cut the pastry in half crossways and then into 1 cm (1/2 inch) wide strips. Twist the strips and place on greased baking trays. Bake for about 10 minutes, or until golden brown. Store in an airtight container for up to 1 week. Refresh in the oven at 180°C (350°F/Gas 4) for 2–3 minutes, then cool.

Split Pea and Ham Soup

Serves 8

500 g (1 lb 2 oz/2¼ cups) yellow split peas
650 g (1 lb 7 oz) ham bone
2 carrots, chopped
2 celery stalks, chopped
1 onion, chopped
2 bay leaves

1. Rinse the split peas in cold water, then drain. Put the peas, ham bone, carrot, celery, onion, bay leaves and 3 litres (105 fl oz/12 cups) of water in a large saucepan. Cover and bring to the boil. Reduce the heat and simmer, partly covered, for 2 hours, or until the peas are tender. Skim off any scum that rises to the surface.

2. Remove the ham bone and cut the meat from the bone, discarding any fat or skin. Finely chop the ham and set aside. Remove the bay leaves. Cool the soup slightly, then blend in batches in a food processor until smooth, adding a little more water if necessary. Stir in the ham and season with salt and pepper, to taste.

Crab and Cheese Puffs

Makes 60

50 g (1 3/4 oz) butter, cubed
125 ml (4 fl oz/1/2 cup) water
115 g (4 oz) plain (all-purpose) flour, sifted
3 eggs, lightly beaten
165 g (5 3/4 oz/1 cup) frozen crab meat, thawed
50 g (1 3/4 oz/1/2 cup) grated cheddar cheese
2 tablespoons snipped chives
1/2 teaspoon sweet paprika
oil, for deep-frying
chilli sprigs, to garnish (optional)
plum sauce, to serve

1. Put the butter and water in a saucepan. Stir the mixture over low heat for 3 minutes, or until the butter has melted. Bring to the boil. Remove from the heat and add the flour all at once. Using a wooden spoon, beat the mixture until smooth. Return to the heat and cook, stirring constantly, for 5 minutes, or until the mixture comes away from the side and base of the pan. Remove from the heat and set aside to cool slightly.
2. Transfer the mixture to a small mixing bowl. Gradually add the eggs, beating constantly until the mixture is glossy. Add the crab meat, grated cheese, chives and paprika, and mix well.
3. Heat the oil in a frying pan. Lower 1 heaped teaspoon of the mixture at a time into the hot oil. Cook the puffs in batches, turning constantly, until they are well puffed up and golden brown. Remove the puffs with a slotted spoon and drain on paper towels. Garnish the crab puffs with fresh chilli sprigs and serve with plum sauce.

Chicken Balls

Makes about 50

1 kg (2 lb 4 oz) minced (ground) chicken
80 g (2¾ oz/1 cup) fresh breadcrumbs
4 spring onions (scallions), sliced
1 tablespoon ground coriander
1 large handful chopped coriander (cilantro) leaves
60 ml (2 fl oz/¼ cup) sweet chilli sauce
1–2 tablespoons lemon juice
oil, for pan-frying

1. Preheat the oven to 200°C (400°F/Gas 6). Mix the mince and breadcrumbs in a large bowl. Add the spring onion, ground and fresh coriander, chilli sauce and lemon juice, to taste, and mix well. With wet hands, form into evenly shaped walnut-sized balls.
2. Fill a deep frying pan with 3 cm (1¼ inches) oil and heat to 180°C (350°F), or until a cube of bread browns in 15 seconds. Pan-fry the balls in batches over high heat until golden. Bake on a baking tray for 5 minutes, or until cooked through.

Zucchini Spirals

Makes 25

2 zucchini (courgettes), coarsely grated
1 small onion, grated
60 g (2^1/4 oz) salami, finely chopped
1 clove garlic, crushed
50 g (1^3/4 oz/^{1}/2 cup) grated parmesan cheese
4 sheets ready-made filo pastry
60 g (2^1/4 oz) butter, melted
35 g (1^1/4 oz/^{1}/3 cup) dried breadcrumbs

1. Grease two oven trays. Combine the zucchini, onion, salami, garlic and cheese in a mixing bowl.
2. Layer the pastry sheets together, lightly brushing each sheet with butter. Spread the zucchini mixture over the pastry, leaving a 5 cm (2 inch) border along one long side; sprinkle breadcrumbs evenly over zucchini mixture.
3. Roll the pastry up tightly over the filling toward the side with the border. Brush all over with the remaining butter. Cover with plastic wrap and refrigerate for 1 hour. Preheat oven to 210°C (415°F/Gas 6–7).
4. Using a sharp knife, cut the roll into 25 slices. Arrange the slices on the prepared trays. Bake for 15 minutes or until spirals are crisp and well browned. Remove from the oven and allow to cool on the trays.

Grilled Figs in Prosciutto

Makes 12

25 g (1 oz) unsalted butter
1 tablespoon orange juice
12 small fresh figs
12 sage leaves
6 prosciutto slices, trimmed and halved lengthways

1. Put the butter in a small heavy-based saucepan. Melt over low heat, then cook the butter for 8–10 minutes, or until the froth subsides and the milk solids appear as brown specks on the bottom of the saucepan. Strain the butter into a clean bowl by pouring it through a strainer lined with a clean tea towel or paper towel. Stir the orange juice into the strained butter.
2. Gently cut a cross in the crown of each fig, cutting two-thirds of the way through. Gently squeeze the base—the top will open like a flower. Sit a sage leaf in the opening of each fig, then wrap a piece of prosciutto around each one, with the ends tucked under the bottom of the fig. Arrange the figs, cut-side-up, on a baking tray and brush lightly with the butter mixture.
3. Move the grill tray to its lowest position, then heat the grill (broiler) to hot. Put the tray of figs on the grill tray and cook for 1–1½ minutes, or until the prosciutto is slightly crispy. Serve warm or at room temperature.

Stilton Soup

Serves 4–6

THYME PITTA CROUTONS
2 large pitta breads
1 1/2 tablespoons finely chopped thyme leaves
50 g (1 3/4 oz/1/2 cup) grated parmesan cheese
30 g (1 oz) butter
2 leeks, white part only, chopped

1 kg (2 lb 4 oz) boiling potatoes, chopped into cubes
1.25 litres (44 fl oz/5 cups) ready-made chicken stock
125 ml (4 fl oz/1/2 cup) cream (whipping)
100 g (3 1/2 oz) stilton cheese
thyme sprigs, to garnish

1. Preheat the oven to 180°C (350°F/Gas 4). To make the croutons, split each pitta bread into two, then cut each half into 8 wedges. Put on baking trays, sprinkle with the combined thyme and parmesan and bake in batches for 5–8 minutes each batch, or until golden.
2. Melt the butter in a large saucepan, add the leek and cook until softened. Add the potato and stock and bring to the boil. Simmer, covered, for 15 minutes, or until the potato is tender (pierce with the point of a knife—if the potato comes away easily, it is cooked).
3. Transfer the mixture, in batches if necessary, to a blender or food processor and blend until smooth. Return to the saucepan and add the cream and cheese, to taste. Stir over low heat until the cheese has melted, being careful not to let the mixture boil. Ladle into individual dishes and garnish with sprigs of fresh thyme. Serve with the thyme pitta croutons.

Smoked Cod Frittata

Makes 12

500 g (1 lb 2 oz) smoked cod
250 ml (9 fl oz/1 cup) milk
8 eggs
65 g (2$^1/_4$ oz/$^2/_3$ cup) grated parmesan cheese
60 g (2$^1/_4$ oz/$^1/_2$ cup) grated cheddar cheese
2 tablespoons chopped thyme
1 large handful basil, torn
2 tablespoons olive oil

1. Put the smoked cod in a saucepan with the milk and enough water to cover. Bring to the boil, then reduce the heat and simmer for about 3–4 minutes. Remove the cod with a slotted spoon and flake the flesh.
2. Whisk the eggs in a bowl and add the cheeses, thyme, basil and the fish. Mix together well.
3. Heat the oil in a 23–25 cm (9–10 inch) heavy-based frying pan. Pour in the mixture and cook over medium heat for 10 minutes, or until set. Put under a hot grill (broiler) for 3–4 minutes, or until just set and lightly golden. Cut into wedges for serving.

Bacon and Onion Mini Quiches

Makes 24

2 sheets frozen shortcrust pastry, thawed
2 teaspoons oil
1 large onion, finely chopped
125 g (4 1/2 oz) bacon slices, finely chopped
3 teaspoons wholegrain mustard
2 eggs
125 ml (4 fl oz/1/2 cup) milk

1. Preheat the oven to 200°C (400°F/Gas 6). Lightly grease 24 mini tart tins. Lay the pastry sheets on a work surface and cut out 24 shapes to fit the tins. Line the tins with the pastry.
2. Heat the oil in a large saucepan over low–medium heat. Add the onion and cook for about 30 minutes, or until golden (caramelized onion needs to be slow-cooked to bring out the sweetness, so don't rush this step). Transfer to a bowl to cool.
3. Add the bacon to the pan and cook until crisp. Add to the onion, stir in the mustard and season to taste with pepper. Spoon a small amount into each pastry case.
4. Beat the eggs with the milk and pour over the onion and bacon mixture. Bake for 15–20 minutes, or until puffed and golden. Remove from the tins while warm and cool on wire racks.

Eggnog Custard Roast Turkey Pudding Fr

Mains

Cake Cranberry Sauce Orange Glazed Ham

Roast Beef with Yorkshire Pudding

Serves 6

2 kg (4 lb 8 oz) sirloin beef on the bone
1/2 teaspoon dry mustard
1/2 teaspoon pepper
50 g vegetable oil or dripping
Yorkshire puddings (see page 97), to serve
gravy (see page 139), to serve

1. Preheat the oven to 180°C (350°F/Gas 4). Trim the meat and score the fat. Mix together the mustard, pepper and salt to taste, and rub all over the meat. Tie the meat, at regular intervals, securely with string, so that it retains its shape as it cooks. Heat the oil or dripping in a frying pan. Add the meat, fat-side-down, and seal quickly. Brown on all sides.
2. Place the meat on a rack in a roasting tin, fat-side-up. Roast the beef 20–25 minutes for rare, 25–30 minutes for medium, or 30–35 minutes for well done. Cover the meat with foil and allow to stand for 15 minutes before carving.
3. Meanwhile, make the Yorkshire puddings. Serve the roast beef with gravy and the puddings.

Roast Turkey

Serves 6–8

3 kg (6 lb 12 oz) whole turkey
1 quantity stuffing (see pages 140–151)
2 tablespoons oil
500 ml (17 fl oz/2 cups) ready-made chicken stock
2 tablespoons plain (all-purpose) flour

1. Remove the neck and giblets from inside the turkey. Wash the turkey well and pat dry inside and out with paper towels. Preheat the oven to 180°C (350°F/Gas 4).
2. Make the stuffing you prefer and loosely stuff into the turkey cavity. Tuck the wings underneath and join the cavity with a skewer. Tie the legs together. Place on a rack in a baking dish. Roast for 2 hours, basting with the combined oil and 125 ml (4 fl oz/1/2 cup) of the stock. Cover the breast and legs with foil after 1 hour if the turkey is overbrowning. Remove from the oven, cover and leave to rest for 15 minutes.
3. To make the gravy, drain off all except 2 tablespoons of the meat juices from the baking dish. Place the dish on the stove over low heat, add the flour and stir well. Stir over medium heat until browned. Gradually add the remaining stock, stirring until the gravy boils and thickens. Serve the turkey with gravy and roast vegetables.

Glazed Ham

Serves 20

7 kg (16 lb) leg of ham
1 large orange
500 ml (17 fl oz/2 cups) water
about 60 cloves
275 g (9$^3/_4$ oz/$^1/_2$ cup) soft brown sugar
1 tablespoon dry mustard
350 g (12 oz/1 cup) golden (dark corn) syrup
1 teaspoon yellow mustard seeds

MUSTARD CREAM
2 tablespoons French mustard
125 g (4$^1/_2$ oz/$^1/_2$ cup) sour cream
120 ml (4 fl oz/$^1/_2$ cup) double (thick) cream

1. Preheat the oven to 180°C (350°F/Gas 4). Remove the rind from the ham by placing your thumb underneath the rind and running your thumb around the edge of the ham. Begin pulling from the widest edge. When the rind has been removed to within 10 cm of the shank end, cut through it and around the shank. Using a sharp knife, remove the excess fat. Squeeze the orange juice and reserve. Peel the rind into long thin strips. Place the ham on a roasting rack in a deep roasting tin. Add the water, orange rind and 6 cloves to the tin. Cover the ham and roasting tin securely with foil and cook for 2 hours.
2. Remove the roasting tin from the oven. Drain the meat and reserve 250 ml (9 fl oz/1 cup) of the meat juices. With a sharp knife, score across the outside fat of the ham with deep cuts crossways and

then diagonally to form a diamond pattern. Mix together the sugar, mustard and golden syrup to a thick paste. Spread half the paste thickly over the ham. Return to the oven; increase the temperature to 220°C (425°F/Gas 7) and cook, uncovered, for 3 minutes.

3 Mix together the reserved orange juice, the mustard seeds and remaining sugar paste to make the glaze. Remove the ham from the oven and brush with a little of the glaze. Press a clove into each diamond. Return the ham to the oven and roast, uncovered, for a further 1 hour, brushing with the glaze every 10 minutes.

4 Place the reserved cooking juices and any remaining glaze in a small saucepan over a low heat and stir until the mixture comes to the boil. Continue to boil, without stirring, for 3 minutes. Remove the pan from the heat and set aside.

5 To make the mustard cream, place the French mustard, sour cream and cream in a bowl and stir well to combine thoroughly. Cover and set aside for 1 hour. Slice the ham and serve warm or cold with the glaze and mustard cream.

Baked Salmon

Serves 8

2 kg (4 lb 8 oz) whole Atlantic salmon, cleaned, gutted and scaled
2 spring onions (scallions), roughly chopped
3 sprigs dill
1/2 lemon, thinly sliced
6 black peppercorns
60 ml (2 fl oz/1/4 cup) dry white wine
3 bay leaves

1. Preheat the oven to 180°C (350°F/Gas 4). If the salmon is too long for your baking dish, remove the head. Rinse the salmon under cold running water and pat dry inside and out with paper towels. Stuff the cavity with the spring onion, dill, lemon slices and peppercorns.
2. Brush a large double-layered piece of foil with oil and lay the salmon on the foil. Sprinkle the wine all over the salmon and arrange the bay leaves over the top. Fold the foil over and wrap up tightly.
3. Bake in a shallow baking dish for 30 minutes. Turn the oven off and leave the salmon in the oven for 45 minutes with the door closed. Do not open or remove the foil during the cooking or standing time.
4. Undo the foil and carefully peel away the skin of the salmon on the top side. Carefully flip the salmon onto the serving plate and remove the skin from the other side. Pull out the fins and any visible bones. Serve at room temperature with lemon slices. This dish also goes very well with tarragon mayonnaise (see page 134).

Baked Veal with Stuffing

Serves 6

1.8 kg (3 lb 10 oz) shoulder of veal, boned and butterflied (ask your butcher to do this)
1 tablespoon olive oil
1 quantity spicy chicken stuffing (see page 146)

1. Preheat the oven to 180°C (350°F/Gas 4). Trim the veal of excess fat and sinew. Place the veal, flesh-side-up, on a board.
2. Spread the stuffing over the flattened veal, then roll up and tie securely with kitchen string. Brush the veal well with a tablespoon of olive oil and season with salt and pepper. Place on a rack in a baking dish. Pour 375 ml (13 fl oz/1 1/2 cups) water into the baking dish.
3. Bake for 1 1/2 hours for medium, or until cooked to your liking. Add extra water to the pan as necessary and skim fat from the surface. Remove the veal from the dish, cover and set aside for 10 minutes before removing the string and carving.
4. Drain any excess fat from the pan juices and boil the juices on the stovetop for 2–5 minutes, or until reduced by about half. Strain, then season, to taste, and serve with the sliced veal.

Roast Goose

Serves 6

3 kg (6 lb 12 oz) whole fresh or frozen goose
1 tablespoon plain (all-purpose) flour
2 tablespoons brandy
375 ml (13 fl oz/1½ cups) ready-made chicken stock
bread sauce (see page 133), for serving

1. If using a frozen goose, thaw in the refrigerator—it may take 1–2 days. Preheat the oven to 180°C (350°F/Gas 4). Remove any excess fat from inside the cavity of the goose. Place the goose in a large pan, cover with boiling water, then drain. Dry thoroughly with paper towels.
2. Place the goose, breast-side-down, on a rack in a very large baking dish. (Make sure the goose doesn't sit directly on the dish or it will be very greasy.) Using a fine skewer, prick the skin of the goose all over, being careful to pierce only the skin, not the flesh.
3. Bake the goose for 1 hour, then remove from the oven and drain off any excess fat. Turn the goose over and bake for another 30 minutes, or until the outside is golden and crisp. Remove from the baking dish, cover loosely with foil and leave for 5–10 minutes.
4. To make the gravy, drain all except 2 tablespoons of fat from the baking dish and place the dish on the stove over low heat. Add the flour and stir to incorporate all the sediment. Stir constantly over medium heat until well browned, without burning. Remove from the heat and gradually stir in the brandy and chicken stock. Return the dish to the heat and stir constantly, until the gravy boils and thickens. Season with salt and pepper, and serve with bread sauce.

Ballotine of Turkey

Serves 8

50 g (1 3/4 oz) butter
1 red onion, finely chopped
3 garlic cloves, crushed
10 prosciutto slices, finely chopped
200 g (7 oz) button mushrooms, chopped
2 tablespoons chopped sage leaves
2 teaspoons finely grated lemon zest
125 g (4 1/2 oz/1 1/2 cups) fresh breadcrumbs
4 kg (9 lb) turkey, fully boned

1. Preheat the oven to 180°C (350°F/Gas 4).
2. To make the stuffing, melt the butter in a large frying pan. Add the onion and cook for 2–3 minutes, or until softened. Add the garlic, prosciutto, mushroom and sage and cook for 3 minutes, stirring occasionally. Transfer to a bowl and stir in the lemon zest, breadcrumbs and salt, to taste. Remove from the heat and allow to cool.
3. Put the turkey on a flat surface and open it out. Pat dry with paper towels. Pound the thicker parts with a rolling pin to flatten the turkey to an even thickness. Spread the stuffing into a log shape near the bottom edge of the turkey, leaving a 2 cm (3/4 inch) border at either side. Roll the turkey up tightly, then truss at regular intervals with kitchen string. Secure the ends with toothpicks to seal the stuffing in.
4. Grease a large piece of foil and roll the turkey up securely inside it, sealing the ends well. Bake on a baking tray for 1 1/2 hours, or until the juices run clear when tested with a skewer. Rest for 10 minutes before removing the foil, toothpicks and string. Cut into slices to serve.

Minted Racks of Lamb

Serves 4

4 x 4-cutlet racks of lamb
300 g (10 1/2 oz/1 cup) mint jelly
2 tablespoons white wine
3 tablespoons finely snipped chives

1. Preheat the oven to 200°C (400°F/Gas 6). Trim any excess fat from the lamb, leaving a thin layer of fat, and clean any meat or sinew from the ends of the bones using a small sharp knife. Cover the bones with foil. Place on a rack in a baking dish.
2. Mix the mint jelly and white wine together in a small pan over high heat. Bring to the boil and boil for 4 minutes, or until the mixture is reduced and thickened. Cool slightly, add the chives, then brush over the racks of lamb. Bake for 15–20 minutes for rare, or 35 minutes if you prefer medium-rare, brushing with glaze every 10 minutes. Remove the foil and leave the lamb to stand for 5 minutes before serving.

Beef Wellington

Serves 6–8

1.25 kg (2 lb 12 oz) beef fillet in one piece
1 tablespoon oil
125 g (4 1/2 oz) firm chicken liver pâté (see page 20), discard jelly
60 g (2 1/4 oz/2/3 cup) button mushrooms, sliced
375 g (13 oz) block ready-made puff pastry, thawed
1 egg, lightly beaten

1. Preheat the oven to 210°C (415°F/Gas 6–7). Grease a large baking tray. Trim the beef of any excess fat and sinew. Fold the thinner part of the tail end under and tie the meat securely with kitchen string at regular intervals to form an even shape.
2. Rub the meat with freshly ground black pepper. Heat the oil over high heat in a large frying pan. Add the meat and brown well all over. Remove from the heat and allow to cool. Remove the string.
3. Spread the pâté over the top and sides of the beef and press the mushrooms into the pâté. Roll the block pastry out on a lightly floured surface to a rectangle large enough to completely enclose the beef.
4. Place the beef on the pastry and fold over to enclose the meat completely, brushing the edges of the pastry with the beaten egg to seal, and folding in the ends. Put the beef onto the baking tray so the seam is underneath. Cut leaf shapes from any extra pastry and use to decorate the top. Use the egg to stick the shapes on.
5. Cut a few slits in the top of the pastry to allow the steam to escape. Brush the top and sides of the pastry with egg, and cook 1 hour for medium. Leave for 10 minutes before cutting into slices and serving.

Blue Cheese and Onion Flan

Serves 8

2 tablespoons olive oil
1 kg (2 lb 4 oz) onions, very thinly sliced
1 teaspoon soft brown sugar
185 g (6 1/2 oz/1 1/2 cups) plain (all-purpose) flour
100 g (3 1/2 oz) butter, chilled and cubed
185 ml (6 fl oz/3/4 cup) cream (whipping)
3 eggs
100 g (3 1/2 oz) blue cheese, crumbled
1 teaspoon chopped thyme leaves

1. Heat the oil in a heavy-based frying pan over low heat and cook the onion and sugar for 45 minutes, or until the onion is caramelized.
2. Sift the flour into a large bowl and rub in the butter with your fingertips until the mixture resembles fine breadcrumbs. Make a well in the centre and add 3–4 tablespoons cold water. Mix with a flat-bladed knife, using a cutting action, until the mixture comes together in beads. Gently gather together and lift onto a lightly floured work surface. Press into a ball, wrap in plastic wrap and refrigerate for 30 minutes.
3. Preheat the oven to 180°C (350°F/Gas 4). Lightly grease a 22 cm (8 1/2 inch) round, loose-based flan (tart) tin. Roll out the pastry on a lightly floured surface to fit the tin. Put the pastry over the tin and press to fit with a small ball of pastry, allowing excess to hang over the side. Trim any excess pastry, then chill for 10 minutes. Line the pastry shell with baking paper and fill with baking beads or uncooked rice. Bake on a baking tray for 10 minutes. Remove the beads and paper, then bake for 10 minutes, or until lightly golden and dry.

4 Cool, then gently spread the onion over the base of the pastry. Whisk the cream in a bowl with the eggs, blue cheese, thyme and some pepper. Pour over the onion and bake for 35 minutes, or until firm. Serve warm or cold.

The type of blue cheese used will alter the flavour of the flan. Types of blue cheeses that can be used include Roquefort, Stilton, Gorgonzola and Bresse Bleu.

Dressed Crab

Serves 1–2

1 kg (2 lb 4 oz) live mud crab
2–3 teaspoons lemon juice
1 1/2 tablespoons whole-egg mayonnaise
80 g (2 3/4 oz/1 cup) fresh breadcrumbs
1 teaspoon worcestershire sauce
2 eggs, hard-boiled
2 tablespoons chopped parsley
1 tablespoon snipped chives

1. Freeze the crab for about 1 hour to immobilize it, then drop it into a large saucepan of boiling water. Reduce the heat and simmer for 10–15 minutes, or until bright orange all over—it should be cooked through by this stage. Drain and cool.
2. Twist the claws off the crab. Pull back the small flap on the underside of the crab and prise off the top shell. Scrape out any creamy brown meat and set aside. Wash and dry the top shell and set aside. Remove the intestines and grey feathery gills from the main body and discard. Scrape out any remaining creamy brown meat and add to the rest. Cut the crab in half and remove the white meat. Crack the claws and remove any meat. Keep the white meat separate.
3. Finely chop the brown crab meat and combine with the lemon juice, mayonnaise and enough of the breadcrumbs to combine. Add the worcestershire sauce and salt and pepper, to taste.
4. Press the egg yolks and whites separately through a sieve to break apart.

5 Place the white crab meat inside the dry crab shell, on both the outside edges. Spoon the brown meat mixture into the centre of the shell and arrange the combined parsley and chives, sieved yolks and whites in rows over the brown crab meat.

This dish can be served with bread, lemon wedges and extra mayonnaise.When buying fresh crabs, choose ones that seem heavy for their size as they will have the most meat.

Beef with Blue Cheese in Pastry

Serves 8

1 bunch English spinach or 500 g (1 lb 2oz) frozen spinach, thawed
50 g (1$^{3}/_{4}$ oz) butter
1.5 kg (3 lb 5 oz) topside beef, trimmed
2 sheets frozen puff pastry, thawed
200 g (7 oz) blue vein cheese, softened
extra puff pastry, thawed, to decorate (optional)
1 egg, lightly beaten

1. Preheat the oven to 200°C (400°F/Gas 6). To prepare the fresh spinach, remove the stalks and wash the leaves well. If using frozen spinach, squeeze out the excess water.
2. Drop the fresh spinach into boiling water. Cook for 30 seconds or until the leaves are just softened. Drain. Refresh in cold water. Pat dry with kitchen paper. Set aside.
3. Heat the butter in a large pan. Add the meat. Brown on all sides to seal in the juices.
4. Put the pastry on a flat surface. Overlap the edges by 1 cm ($^{1}/_{2}$ inch). Arrange the spinach over the pastry, leaving a 5 cm (2 inch) border. Crumble the cheese over the spinach. Put the beef in the centre of the pastry. Fold in the narrow ends. Fold the remaining pastry over to enclose the beef. Turn the seam to the underside. Decorate with extra pastry. Brush over the pastry with the egg. Cut a few slits in the top of the pastry to allow the steam to escape.
5. Put the beef on a lightly greased baking tray. Bake in the oven for 25–30 minutes, or until the pastry is golden. Let stand, covered with foil, for 10 minutes, before slicing and serving.

Baked Fish with Spices

Serves 2

2 x 300 g (10$^{1}/_{2}$ oz) whole firm white fish
1 onion, chopped
1 garlic clove, crushed
1 teaspoon chopped fresh ginger
1 teaspoon grated lemon zest
2 tablespoons tamarind sauce
1 tablespoon soy sauce
1 tablespoon peanut oil

1. Preheat the oven to 180°C (350°F/Gas 4). Make deep slashes on each side of the fish with a sharp knife. Place the fish on two large sheets of foil.
2. Blend the chopped onion, garlic, ginger, lemon zest, tamarind sauce, soy sauce and peanut oil in a food processor, until smooth.
3. Spread the spice mixture evenly over both sides and on the inside of both fish.
4. Wrap foil loosely around each fish and secure to make neat parcels. Place the parcels in a baking dish and bake for 30 minutes, or until the fish is just cooked through. Serve the parcels so they can be unwrapped, steaming, at the table.

Feta and Olive Herb Pie

Serves 4–6

2 teaspoons sugar
2 teaspoons (7 g/1/4 oz) dried yeast
2 tablespoons olive oil
60 g (2 1/4 oz/1/2 cup) plain (all-purpose) flour
125 g (4 1/2 oz/1 cup) self-raising flour
40 g (1 1/2 oz/1/4 cup) pine nuts, toasted
1 onion, sliced
1 very large handful flat-leaf (Italian) parsley, chopped
1 sprig rosemary, chopped
3 sprigs thyme, chopped
5 fresh basil leaves, torn
1 garlic clove, crushed
175 g (6 oz/1 1/4 cups) crumbled feta cheese
35 g (1 1/4 oz/1/4 cup) pitted olives, chopped

1. Dissolve half the sugar in 125 ml (4 fl oz/1/2 cup) warm water and sprinkle the yeast over the top. Leave for 10 minutes, or until frothy (if it doesn't foam, the yeast is dead and you will need to start again). Then mix the yeast mixture with half the oil.
2. Sift the flours and 1/2 teaspoon salt into a large bowl. Make a well in the centre and pour in the yeast mixture. Mix well and knead on a floured board until smooth. Cut in half, then roll each half into a 20 cm (8 inch) circle. Place one circle on a lightly greased baking tray and the other on a baking paper-covered baking tray. Cover the circles with a cloth and put in a warm place for 10–15 minutes, or until doubled in size.

3. Preheat the oven to 200°C (400°F/Gas 6). Toast the pine nuts by dry-frying them in a frying pan, stirring and watching them constantly so they don't burn. Set aside to cool. Heat the remaining oil in a frying pan and cook the onion for 10 minutes, or until golden brown. Sprinkle with the remaining sugar and cook until caramelized. Transfer to a bowl and mix with the herbs, pine nuts, garlic, feta cheese and olives.
4. Spread the mixture over the pastry on the greased tray. Brush the edge with water and put the second pastry circle on top, using the paper to help lift it over. Press the edges together to seal and pinch together to form a pattern. Cut a few slits in the top to allow steam to escape. Bake for 30–35 minutes, or until crisp and golden brown. Serve warm, cut into wedges.

To toast pine nuts, you can dry-fry them in a frying pan, stirring and watching them constantly so they don't burn.

Lobster Thermidor

Serves 2

1 live lobster
65 g (2 1/4 oz) butter
4 spring onions (scallions), finely chopped
2 tablespoons plain (all-purpose) flour
1/2 teaspoon dry mustard
2 tablespoons white wine
250 ml (9 fl oz/1 cup) milk
3 tablespoons thick (double/heavy) cream
1 tablespoon chopped parsley
50 g (1 3/4 oz/1/3 cup) gruyère cheese, grated

1. Freeze the lobster for 1 hour to immobilize. To cook, plunge the lobster into a saucepan of boiling water until the shell just turns red. Allow to cool and cut the lobster in half lengthways.
2. Remove the lobster meat and set aside. Wash the half shells and set aside. Crack the legs and prise the meat from them. Remove the intestinal vein and soft body matter and discard. Slice the lobster meat into 2 cm (3/4 inch) pieces, cover and refrigerate.
3. Melt 50 g (1 3/4 oz) butter in a frying pan. Add the spring onions and cook for 2 minutes or until soft. Add the flour and mustard and cook, stirring, for 1 minute. Gradually add the wine and milk, stirring until the mixture boils and thickens. Simmer for 1 minute. Stir in the cream, parsley and lobster meat and season with salt and pepper.
4. Spoon the mixture into the half shells, sprinkle with the cheese and dot with the remaining butter. Cook under a prepared grill (broiler) for 2 minutes, or until lightly browned. Garnish with lemon slices to serve.

Tuna Steaks with Olive Paste

Serves 6

125 ml (4 fl oz/1/2 cup) olive oil
2 tablespoons dry white wine
2 tablespoons lemon juice
6 x 200 g (7 oz) tuna steaks
2 tablespoons sour cream

OLIVE PASTE
115 g (4 oz/1 cup) pitted black olives
2 teaspoons capers, rinsed and squeezed dry
1 garlic clove, crushed
1 tablespoon olive oil
1 tablespoon finely chopped parsley

1. Combine the olive oil, white wine and lemon juice in a jar with the lid on and shake vigorously. Place the tuna steaks in a single layer in a shallow baking dish. Pour the marinade over and set aside in the refrigerator for 1 hour, turning the tuna over halfway through.
2. To make the olive paste, combine the olives, capers, garlic and olive oil to form a paste. Transfer the paste to a bowl, cover with plastic wrap and store in the refrigerator until required.
3. Shortly before serving, stir the chopped parsley into the olive paste and set aside for at least 10 minutes at room temperature.
4. Remove the tuna steaks from the dish and reserve the marinade. Place the steaks in a foil-lined grill pan and cook under a preheated grill (broiler) on high heat for 2–3 minutes on each side, basting occasionally with the marinade. Garnish with the olive paste to serve.

Roast Leg of Lamb with Garlic and Rosemary

Serves 6

2 kg (4 lb 8 oz) leg of lamb
2 garlic cloves, cut into thin slivers
2 tablespoons rosemary sprigs
2 teaspoons oil
mint sauce (see page 131), to serve

1. Preheat the oven to 180°C (350°F/Gas 4). Using a small sharp knife, cut small slits all over the lamb. Insert the slivers of garlic and sprigs of rosemary into the slits.
2. Brush the lamb with the oil and sprinkle with salt and black pepper. Place on a rack in a baking dish. Add 125 ml (4 1/2 fl oz/1/2 cup) water to the dish. Bake for about 1 1/2 hours for medium, or until cooked as desired, basting often with the pan juices. Keep warm and leave for 10–15 minutes before carving. Serve with mint sauce.

Poached Ocean Trout

Serves 8–10

2 litres (70 fl oz/8 cups) dry white wine
60 ml (2 fl oz/1/4 cup) white wine vinegar
2 onions
10 whole cloves
4 carrots, chopped
1 lemon, cut into quarters
2 bay leaves
4 sprigs parsley
1 teaspoon whole black peppercorns
2.5 kg (5 lb 8 oz) whole ocean trout, cleaned, gutted and scaled
dill mayonnaise (see page 130), to serve

1 Combine the wine and vinegar with 2.5 litres (80 fl oz) water in a large heavy-based pan.

2 Stud the onions with the cloves. Add to the pan with the carrot, lemon, bay leaves, parsley and peppercorns. Bring to the boil, reduce the heat and simmer for 30–35 minutes. Cool. Strain into a fish kettle (poacher) that will hold the trout.

3 Place the whole fish in the fish kettle and add water if necessary, to just cover the fish. Bring to the boil, then reduce the heat to a low simmer. Cover and poach gently for 10–15 minutes, until the fish flakes when tested in the thickest part. Remove the kettle from the heat and leave the fish to cool in the liquid.

4 Remove the cold fish from the liquid, place on a serving platter and peel back the skin. Garnish with watercress and lemon slices. Serve with dill mayonnaise.

Mushroom Nut Roast with Tomato Sauce

Serves 6

2 tablespoons olive oil
1 large onion, diced
2 garlic cloves, crushed
300 g (10 1/2 oz) mushrooms, finely chopped
200 g (7 oz/1 1/4 cups) raw cashew nuts, finely chopped
200 g (7 oz/1 1/4 cups) brazil nuts, finely chopped
125 g (4 1/2 oz/1 cup) grated cheddar cheese
25 g (1 oz/1/4 cup) freshly grated parmesan cheese
1 egg, lightly beaten
2 tablespoons snipped chives
80 g (2 3/4 oz/1 cup) fresh breadcrumbs

TOMATO SAUCE
1 1/2 tablespoons olive oil
1 onion, finely chopped
1 garlic clove, crushed
400 g (14 oz/1 2/3 cups) tin tomatoes, chopped
1 tablespoon tomato paste (concentrated purée)
1 teaspoon caster (superfine) sugar

1. Grease a 14 x 21 cm (5 1/2 x 8 1/4 inch) loaf (bar) tin and line the base with baking paper.
2. Heat the oil in a frying pan and add the onion, garlic and mushrooms. Fry until soft, then cool.

3. Preheat the oven to 180°C (350°F/Gas 4). Combine the cooled mushroom mixture, chopped nuts, cheddar and parmesan, egg, chives and breadcrumbs in a bowl. Mix well and season, to taste. Press into the tin and bake for 45 minutes, or until firm. Leave for 5 minutes, then turn out and cut into slices.
4. To make the tomato sauce, heat the oil in a saucepan, add the onion and garlic and cook, stirring frequently, for 5 minutes, or until soft but not brown. Stir in the tomato, tomato paste, sugar and 80 ml (2 1/2 fl oz/1/3 cup) water. Simmer gently for 3–5 minutes, or until slightly thickened. Season with salt and pepper. Serve the tomato sauce with the sliced nut roast.

For a variation, use a different mixture of nuts and add some seeds. You can use nuts such as pecans, almonds, hazelnuts (without skins) and pine nuts. Suitable seeds to use include sesame, pumpkin and sunflower seeds.

Game Pie

Serves 4–6

1 kg (2 lb 4 oz) rabbit, boned, cut into bite-sized pieces
1.25 kg (2 lb 12 oz) venison goulash or diced venison
30 g (1 oz/1/4 cup) plain (all-purpose) flour
2–3 tablespoons oil
2 bacon slices, chopped
1 onion, sliced into thin wedges
2 garlic cloves, crushed
150 g (5 1/2 oz/1 2/3 cup) button mushrooms, cut in halves
250 ml (9 fl oz/1 cup) red wine
250 ml (9 fl oz/1 cup) ready-made beef stock
3 sprigs thyme
2 bay leaves
550 g (1 lb 4 oz) block ready-made puff pastry, thawed
1 egg yolk
2 tablespoons milk

1. Lightly coat the rabbit and venison in seasoned flour. Heat the oil in a large saucepan and cook the bacon over a medium heat until golden. Remove. Brown the meats well in batches, remove and set aside. Add the onion and the crushed garlic to the saucepan and cook until browned.

2. Return the bacon and meat to the saucepan and add the mushrooms, wine, stock, thyme and bay leaves. Bring to the boil, then reduce the heat and simmer over low heat, stirring occasionally, for 1 1/2 hours, or until the meat is tender. Transfer to a heatproof bowl. Remove the thyme and bay leaves. Refrigerate until cold.

3 Preheat the oven to 200°C (400°F/Gas 6). Spoon the meat mixture into a 2 litre (70 fl oz) ovenproof dish. Roll the pastry on a lightly floured surface to about 5 mm (1/4 inch) thick. Cut strips the width of the pie dish rim and secure to the rim of the dish with a little water. Roll the leftover pastry on a lightly floured surface until large enough to fit the top of the pie dish. Brush the edges of the pastry strips with a little combined egg yolk and milk. Drape the larger pastry over the rolling pin and lower it onto the top of the pie. Trim off any excess pastry using a sharp knife. Score the edges of the pastry with the back of a knife to seal. Use any leftover pastry to decorate the top. Cut two slits in the top of the pastry and brush all over with the remaining egg and milk mixture. Bake for 30–40 minutes, or until puffed and golden.

You can ask your butcher to bone the rabbit. Order the venison from the butcher or poultry shop.

Mushrooms with Bean Purée, Puy Lentils and Red Wine Sauce

Serves 4

4 large field mushrooms
1 tablespoon olive oil
1 red onion, cut into thin wedges
3 garlic cloves, crushed
200 g (7 oz/1 cup) puy green lentils
185 ml (6 fl oz/3/4 cup) red wine
435 ml (15 1/4 fl oz/1 3/4 cups) ready-made vegetable stock
1 tablespoon finely chopped flat-leaf (Italian) parsley
30 g (1 oz) butter

BEAN PURÉE
1 large potato, cut into chunks
2 tablespoons extra virgin olive oil
400 g (14 oz/2 cups) tinned cannellini beans, drained and rinsed
2 large garlic cloves, crushed
1 tablespoon ready-made vegetable stock

RED WINE SAUCE
170 ml (5 1/2 fl oz/2/3 cup) red wine
2 tablespoons tomato paste (concentrated purée)
375 ml (13 fl oz/1 1/2 cups) ready-made vegetable stock
1 tablespoon soft brown sugar

1. Finely chop the mushroom stalks and set aside the mushroom caps.
2. Heat the oil in a large saucepan, add the onion and cook over medium heat for 2–3 minutes, or until soft. Add 1 clove of the garlic

and the mushroom stalks and cook for 1 minute. Stir in the lentils, red wine and vegetable stock and bring to the boil. Reduce the heat and simmer, covered, for 20–25 minutes, stirring occasionally, or until the liquid is reduced and the lentils are cooked. If the mixture is too wet, uncover and boil until slightly thick. Stir in the parsley. Keep warm.

3. To make the bean purée, bring a small saucepan of water to the boil over high heat and cook the potato for 4–5 minutes, or until tender (pierce with the point of a sharp knife—if the knife comes away easily, the potato is cooked). Drain and mash with a potato masher or fork until smooth. Stir in half the extra virgin olive oil and set aside. Combine the cannellini beans and garlic in a food processor. Add the stock and remaining oil and process until smooth. Transfer to a bowl and fold the mashed potato through. Keep warm.

4. Melt the butter in a deep frying pan. Add the remaining garlic and the mushrooms caps and cook in batches over medium heat for 3–4 minutes each side, or until the mushrooms are tender. Set aside and keep warm.

5. To make the sauce, add the red wine to the same frying pan, then scrape the bottom to release any sediment. Add the combined tomato paste, stock and sugar and bring to the boil. Cook for about 10 minutes, or until reduced and thick.

6. Place the mushrooms on individual serving plates and top with warm bean purée. Spoon some lentil mixture over the top and drizzle with the red wine sauce. Season and serve.

Pork with Apple and Prune Stuffing

Serves 8

1 green apple, chopped
90 g (3¼ oz/⅓ cup) chopped pitted prunes
2 tablespoons port
1 tablespoon chopped parsley
2 kg (4 lb 9 oz) pork loin, boned
olive oil and salt, to rub on pork
gravy (see page 139), for serving

1. Preheat the oven to 240°C (475°F/Gas 9). To make the stuffing, combine the apple, prunes, port and parsley. Lay the pork loin on a board with the rind underneath. Spread the stuffing over the meat side of the loin, roll up and secure with skewers or string at regular intervals. If some of the filling falls out while tying, carefully push it back in. Score the pork rind with a sharp knife at 1 cm (½ inch) intervals (if the butcher hasn't already done so) and rub generously with oil and salt.

2. Put the pork on a rack in a baking dish. Bake for 15 minutes, then reduce the heat to 180°C (350°F/Gas 4) and bake for 1½–2 hours, or until the pork is cooked through. The juices will run clear when a skewer is inserted into the thickest part of the meat. Cover and stand for 15 minutes before removing the skewers or string and carving. Reserve any pan juices for making the gravy.

3. If the rind fails to crackle, carefully remove it from the meat, cutting between the fat layer and the meat. Scrape off any excess fat and put the rind on a piece of foil. Place under a moderate grill (broiler), and grill until the rind has crackled. Serve with gravy.

Quails with Bacon and Rosemary

Serves 4

8 quails
1 onion, chopped
3 bacon slices, chopped
1 tablespoon rosemary leaves
30 g (1 oz) butter, melted
125 ml (4 fl oz/1/2 cup) port
125 ml (4 fl oz/1/2 cup) cream (whipping)
1 teaspoon cornflour

1. Preheat the oven to 200°C (400°F/Gas 6). Wash the quails thoroughly under cold running water, then dry thoroughly inside and out with paper towels. Tuck the wings underneath the quails and tie the legs close to the body with kitchen string.
2. Spread the onion, bacon and rosemary over the base of a baking dish, and add the quails. Brush each one with melted butter. Combine the port with 60 ml (2 fl oz/1/4 cup) of water, then pour 125 ml (4 fl oz/1/2 cup) of this mixture over the quails.
3. Bake for about 25 minutes, or until the juices run clear when the quails are pierced in the thigh with a skewer. Cover and leave for 10 minutes in a warm place.
4. Carefully strain any juices from the baking dish into a small saucepan, reserving the rosemary and bacon mixture. Add the remaining port and water mixture to the pan and bring to the boil. Reduce the heat and gradually stir in the blended cream and cornflour, stirring until the mixture boils and is slightly thickened. Serve the quails with the sauce and the reserved rosemary and bacon mixture.

Roast Chicken with Bacon and Sage Stuffing

Serves 6

2 x 1.25 kg (2 lb 12 oz) whole chickens
2 tablespoons oil
1 small onion, finely chopped
4 bacon slices, finely chopped
1 tablespoon chopped sage
125 g (4 1/2 oz/1 1/2 cups) fresh breadcrumbs
1 egg, lightly beaten
gravy (see page 139), to serve

1. Preheat the oven to 180°C (350°F/Gas 4). Remove the giblets and any large fat deposits from the chickens. Wipe over and pat dry inside and out with paper towels.
2. Finely chop two of the bacon slices. Heat half the oil in a small frying pan. Add the onion and bacon and cook until the onion is soft and the bacon is starting to brown. Transfer to a bowl and cool. Add the sage, breadcrumbs and egg to the onion, season, to taste, and mix lightly. Spoon some stuffing into each chicken cavity.
3. Fold the wings back and tuck them under the chickens. Tie the legs of each chicken together with string. Put the chickens on a rack in a large baking dish, making sure they are not touching, and brush with the remaining oil. Pour 250 ml (9 fl oz/1 cup) water into the baking dish.
4. Cut the remaining bacon into long, thin strips and lay across the chicken breasts. Brush the bacon with oil. Bake for 45–60 minutes, or until the juices run clear when a thigh is pierced with a skewer. Serve with gravy.

Roast Sirloin with Mustard Sauce

Serves 6

1.5 kg (3 lb 5 oz) beef sirloin
90 g (3 1/4 oz/1/3 cup) wholegrain mustard
1 tablespoon dijon mustard
1 teaspoon honey
1 garlic clove, crushed
1 tablespoon oil
honey mustard sauce (see page 129), to serve

1. Preheat the oven to 220°C (425°F/Gas 7). Cut most of the fat from the piece of beef sirloin, leaving a thin layer.
2. Mix together the mustards and add the honey and garlic. Spread evenly over the sirloin in a thick layer.
3. Place the oil in a baking dish and heat it in the oven for 2 minutes. Place the meat in the hot dish and roast for 15 minutes.
4. Reduce the oven temperature to 200°C (400°F/Gas 6) and cook for about 40 minutes for rare, 45–50 minutes for medium rare and 60–65 minutes for well done. Remove from the oven, cover the meat and set aside for 10–15 minutes before carving. Meanwhile, make the honey mustard sauce and serve.

Roast Duck with Orange Sauce

Serves 4

2 kg (4 lb 8 oz) duck, with neck
2 chicken wings, chopped
125 ml (4 1/2 fl oz/1/2 cup) white wine
1 onion, chopped
1 carrot, sliced
1 tomato, chopped
bouquet garni (a bay leaf and small sprigs of parsley, thyme and marjoram, tied together)

ORANGE SAUCE
2 tablespoons grated orange zest
170 ml (5 1/2 fl oz/2/3 cup) orange juice
80 ml (2 1/2 fl oz/1/3 cup) Cointreau
2 teaspoons cornflour

1. Place the duck neck, chicken wings and wine in a pan. Boil over high heat for 5 minutes, or until the wine has reduced by half. Add the onion, carrot, tomato, bouquet garni and 500 ml (17 fl oz/2 cups) of water. Bring to the boil and simmer gently for 40 minutes. Strain and set aside 250 ml (9 fl oz/1 cup) of the stock.

2. Preheat the oven to 180°C (350°F/Gas 4). Place the duck in a large saucepan, cover with boiling water, then drain. Dry with paper towels. With a fine skewer, prick all over the outside of the duck, piercing only the skin, not the flesh. Place the duck, breast-side-down, on a rack in a baking dish and bake for 50 minutes.

3 Drain off any fat, turn the duck over and pour the reserved stock into the pan. Bake for 40 minutes, or until the breast is golden brown. Remove the duck from the pan and leave in a warm place for 15 minutes before carving. Reserve any meat juices for making the orange sauce.

4 To make the orange sauce, skim any fat off the reserved meat juices. Place in a saucepan with the zest, juice and Cointreau and bring to the boil. Reduce the heat and simmer for 5 minutes. Blend the cornflour with 1 tablespoon water, add to the sauce and stir over heat until the mixture boils and thickens. Serve the orange sauce with the duck.

You may need to order your duck in advance from a game specialist or poulterer. Some large supermarkets have them. If desired, rub a little salt into the skin of the duck for added crispness.

Roast Pheasant and Apples

Serves 4–6

2 x 1 kg (2 lb 4 oz) pheasants
6 bacon slices
8 sprigs thyme
2 large pieces of muslin (cheesecloth)
80 g (2 3/4 oz) butter, melted
2 apples, cored and cut into thick wedges
60 ml (2 fl oz/1/4 cup) apple cider
125 ml (4 fl oz/1/2 cup) cream (whipping)
2 teaspoons thyme leaves
2–4 teaspoons apple cider vinegar

1. Preheat the oven to 230°C (450°C/Gas 8). Rinse the pheasants and pat dry. Tie the legs together with string and tuck the wings under. Wrap 3 bacon slices around each pheasant and secure with toothpicks. Thread the thyme sprigs through the bacon. Dip the pieces of muslin into the melted butter and wrap one around each pheasant.

2. Place on a rack in a baking dish and bake for 10 minutes. Reduce the oven to 200°C (400°C/Gas 6) and bake for another 35 minutes. About 20 minutes before the end of the cooking, add the apple wedges to the base of the dish. The pheasants are cooked when the juices run clear when the pheasants are pricked with a skewer. Remove the pheasants and apple wedges, discard the muslin and toothpicks, then cover and keep warm while making the sauce.

3 Place the baking dish with the juices on the stovetop. Pour the apple cider into the pan and bring to the boil. Cook for 3 minutes, or until reduced by half. Scrape the base of the pan to lift any sticky pan juices. Strain into a small clean saucepan. Add the cream to the saucepan and boil for 5 minutes, or until the sauce thickens slightly. Stir in the thyme leaves and season well with salt and freshly cracked black pepper. Add the apple cider vinegar, to taste. Serve with the pheasant and apple.

The buttered muslin and bacon help protect the delicate breast meat from drying out. Do not overcook the pheasant as it may dry out. Traditionally pheasant was served while still pink but most people today prefer it to be cooked through for safety.

Roast Pork Fillet and Glazed Apples

Serves 4

750 g (1 lb 10 oz) pork fillet
30 g (1 oz) butter
1 tablespoon oil
1 garlic clove, crushed
1/2 teaspoon grated fresh ginger
1 tablespoon wholegrain mustard
60 ml (2 fl oz/1/4 cup) apple sauce (see page 128)
2 tablespoons ready-made chicken stock
125 ml (4 fl oz/1/2 cup) cream (whipping)
1 teaspoon cornflour

GLAZED APPLES
2 green apples, cored
50 g (1 3/4 oz) butter
2 tablespoons soft brown sugar

1. Preheat the oven to 180°C (350°F/Gas 4). Trim the pork fillet, removing any fat or sinew from the outside. Tie the fillet with kitchen string at 3 cm (1 1/4 inch) intervals to keep in shape. Heat the butter and oil in a frying pan, add the pork fillet and cook until browned all over. Remove and place on a rack in a baking dish. (Retain the cooking oils in the frying pan.) Add 125 ml (4 fl oz/1/2 cup) water to the baking dish and bake for 15–20 minutes. Leave 10 minutes before untying and slicing.
2. To make the sauce, reheat the oils in the frying pan, add the garlic and ginger and stir for 1 minute. Stir in the mustard, apple sauce and stock. Slowly stir in the combined cream and cornflour and stir until the mixture boils and thickens.

3. To make the glazed apples, cut the apples into 1 cm (1/2 inch) slices. Melt the butter in the pan and add the sugar. Stir until the sugar dissolves. Add the apple slices and pan-fry, turning occasionally, until the apples are glazed and lightly browned.
4. Slice the pork and serve the apple and mustard sauce over it. Serve with the glazed apples.

Pork fillets can be thick and short or long and thin and the time they take to cook will vary accordingly.

Roast Rack of Venison

Serves 6–8

MARINADE
250 ml (9 fl oz/1 cup) red wine
60 ml (2 fl oz/1/4 cup) olive oil
2 tablespoons brandy
1 spring onion (scallion) or brown onion, finely chopped
2 garlic cloves, crushed
2 bay leaves
6 juniper berries, crushed
1 tablespoon thyme leaves
8 whole black peppercorns

2 x 10-cutlet racks of venison
250 ml (9 fl oz/1 cup) ready-made beef stock
1 tablespoon redcurrant jelly
2 tablespoons port
40 g (1 1/2 oz) butter, chilled and cubed
150 g (5 1/2 oz/1 cup) tin chestnuts

1. Stir the marinade ingredients together in a large bowl. Coat the venison racks in the marinade. Cover and marinate in the refrigerator overnight, turning occasionally.

2. Preheat the oven to 220°C (425°F/Gas 7). Remove the venison racks from the marinade, reserving the marinade. Roast the racks for 30 minutes for medium, or slightly longer if you prefer well-done meat. Remove from the oven, cover with foil and leave to rest for 10 minutes while you make the sauce.

3. Put the reserved marinade in a small saucepan with the beef stock and bring to the boil over medium heat. Boil until reduced to 250 ml (9 fl oz/1 cup). Reduce the heat, stir in the redcurrant jelly and port and simmer gently. Whisk 30 g (1 oz) butter into the sauce until combined. Remove from the heat.
4. Drain the chestnuts and heat in a small saucepan with the remaining butter. Season with freshly ground black pepper.
5. Carve the racks into chops and serve with the hot chestnuts. Strain the warm sauce through a sieve and serve over the meat. Serve immediately.

Salmon Steaks with Herb Sauce

Serves 4

4 x 250 g (9 oz) salmon steaks
2 tablespoons oil

HERB SAUCE
375 ml (13 fl oz/1 1/2 cups) ready-made fish stock
125 ml (4 fl oz/1/2 cup) white wine
3 tablespoons snipped chives
3 tablespoons chopped parsley
2 tablespoons chopped basil
2 tablespoons chopped tarragon
250 ml (9 fl oz/1 cup) cream (whipping)
2 egg yolks

1. Pat the salmon steaks dry with paper towels.
2. For the herb sauce, combine the stock and wine in a saucepan and bring to the boil. Boil for 5 minutes or until the liquid has reduced by half. Allow to cool and transfer to a food processor, adding the chives, parsley, basil and tarragon and blend for 30 seconds, or until smooth. Return to the pan, then stir in the cream and bring to the boil. Reduce the heat to low and simmer for 5 minutes, or until the sauce has reduced by half. Place the egg yolks in a food processor and blend until smooth. With the motor running, gradually drizzle in the herb mixture. Blend until the sauce is smooth and creamy. Season, to taste.
3. Heat the oil in a frying pan, add the salmon steaks and cook over medium heat for 3 minutes each side, or until just cooked through (do not overcook). Serve hot with herb sauce.

Roast Turkey Breast with Parsley Crust

Serves 8

PARSLEY CRUST
60 g ($2^1/_4$ oz) butter
4 spring onions (scallions), finely chopped
2 garlic cloves, crushed
160 g ($5^3/_4$ oz/2 cups) fresh white breadcrumbs
2 tablespoons finely chopped parsley

1 kg (2 lb 4 oz) whole turkey breast
1 egg, lightly beaten
beetroot relish (see page 135), to serve

1. To make the parsley crust, melt the butter in a small frying pan over medium heat. Add the spring onion and garlic and stir until softened. Add the breadcrumbs and parsley and stir until combined. Allow to cool.
2. Preheat the oven to 180°C (350°F/Gas 4). Place the turkey in a deep baking dish and pat dry with paper towels. Brush with egg.
3. Press the parsley crust firmly onto the turkey. Bake for 45 minutes, or until the crust is lightly golden. Serve sliced with beetroot relish.

Seafood Pie

Serves 8

2 tablespoons olive oil
3 large brown onions, thinly sliced
1 fennel bulb, thinly sliced
600 ml (21 fl oz/2 1/2 cups) ready-made fish stock
750 ml (26 fl oz/3 cups) cream (whipping)
1 tablespoon brandy
750 g (1 lb 10 oz) firm white fish fillets, skinned
250 g (9 oz) scallops
500 g (1 lb 2 oz) raw medium prawns (shrimp)
2 tablespoons chopped flat-leaf (Italian) parsley
2 sheets frozen puff pastry, thawed
1 egg, lightly beaten

1. Preheat the oven to 220°C (425°F/Gas 7). Peel the prawns and gently pull out the dark vein from each prawn back, starting at the head end. Take off each head and tail. Chop the fish into large pieces.
2. Heat the oil in a deep frying pan, add the onion and fennel and cook over medium heat for 20 minutes or until caramelized.
3. Add the stock to the pan and bring to the boil. Cook until the liquid is almost evaporated. Stir in the cream and brandy, bring to the boil, then reduce the heat and simmer for 10 minutes, or until reduced by half. Add the seafood and parsley and toss for 3 minutes, or until the seafood just starts to cook.

4. Lightly grease a $2^1/_2$ litre (87 fl oz) pie dish and add the seafood mixture. Arrange the pastry over the top to cover, trim the excess and press down around the edges. Decorate with any trimmings. Make a steam hole in the top and brush the pastry lightly with beaten egg. Bake for 30 minutes, or until the seafood is cooked through and the pastry is crisp and golden.

Fresh fish fillets should have a fresh odour, firm texture and moist appearance. They should be refrigerated, tightly wrapped and used within a day, or two days at most.

Standing Rib Roast with Pâté

Serves 8

1 bacon slice, chopped
1 small onion, finely chopped
115 g (4 oz/1¼ cups) finely chopped mushrooms
115 g chicken liver pâté (see page 20)
30 g (1 oz/⅓ cup) dry breadcrumbs
2 tablespoons chopped parsley
¼ teaspoon dry mixed herbs
1 egg, lightly beaten
3 kg (6 lb 12 oz) standing rib of beef
gravy (see page 139), to serve

1. Preheat the oven to 220°C (425°F/Gas 7). Place the bacon in a dry frying pan. Heat gently until it is just beginning to soften. Add the onion and mushrooms and cook, stirring constantly, for about 3 minutes until the onion is soft and translucent. Transfer to a bowl. Mix in the pâté, breadcrumbs, parsley, mixed herbs and egg and season to taste with pepper.
2. Cut a slice in the meat between the rib bones and the outer layer of fat at the narrow end. Remove any excess fat. Fill the cavity with the stuffing. Replace the flap and secure with a skewer.
3. Place the meat in a roasting tin, fat-side-up (the bones form a natural rack). Roast for 15 minutes, then reduce the oven temperature to 180°C (350°F/Gas 4). Continue to roast for a further 1–1½ hours, or until done to taste.
4. Remove the meat from the oven, cover with foil and leave to stand for 15 minutes before carving. Serve hot with gravy.

Turkey Buffe

Serves 6–8

2.7 kg (6 oz) turkey buffe (breast on the bone)
rice and fruit stuffing (see page 140)

GLAZE
125 ml (4 fl oz/1/2 cup) orange juice
15 g (1/2 oz) butter
2 teaspoons soft brown sugar

1. Bone the turkey breast and remove the bone from the wings.
2. Lay the turkey flat and spread the stuffing along the centre. Fold the breast inwards and sew the turkey together using a trussing needle and kitchen string. Tuck in the skin at the neck and press the wings in towards the breast. Sew or tie securely with string, or secure well with skewers. Preheat the oven to 180°C (350°F/Gas 4).
3. To make the glaze, stir the orange juice, butter and sugar together in a small pan. Bring to the boil and stir until the sugar is dissolved. Allow to cool.
4. Put the turkey on a rack in a baking dish. Bake for 13/4–2 hours, basting with the glaze. (If the turkey is overbrowning, cover loosely with foil.) When cooked, remove from the oven and cover and set aside for 20 minutes before removing the string or skewers. Slice and serve with the remaining glaze.

Eggnog Custard Roast Turkey Pudding Tra

Sides

ake Cranberry Sauce Orange Glazed Ham

Golden Roast Potatoes

Serves 8

8 medium roasting potatoes
50 g (1 3/4 oz) butter, melted
4 tablespoons olive oil
1/2 teaspoon paprika

1. Preheat the oven to 200°C (400°F/Gas 6). Boil the potatoes for 5 minutes. Drain and pat dry with kitchen paper.
2. Using the prongs of a fork, scrape the potatoes to form a rough surface. Put them in a shallow baking dish. Mix together the melted butter and oil and brush over the potatoes. Sprinkle with paprika. Roast for 20 minutes.
3. Remove the potatoes from the oven and brush with the butter mixture. Roast for a further 20 minutes. Repeat this process and roast for a further 15 minutes. Serve hot.

Hasselback Potatoes

Serves 4

8 medium all-purpose potatoes
20 g (3/4 oz) butter, melted
2 teaspoons dry breadcrumbs
2 teaspoons grated parmesan cheese (optional)

1. Preheat the oven to 180°C (350°F/Gas 4). Lightly grease a baking dish. Wash and peel the potatoes. Cut a slice off the base of each potato so the potato will sit flat. Put each potato cut-side-down on a board and make thin evenly-spaced cuts about two-thirds of the way through each potato.

2. Put the potatoes in the prepared baking dish. Brush the potatoes with the melted butter, then sprinkle with a mixture of the dry breadcrumbs and parmesan cheese. Roast for 40–50 minutes, or until golden brown and tender. Serve hot.

Asparagus with Butter and Parmesan

Serves 6

18 fresh asparagus spears
40 g ($1\frac{1}{2}$ oz) butter, melted
fresh parmesan cheese shavings, to serve

1. Snap any thick woody ends from the asparagus and discard. Peel the bottom half of each spear with a vegetable peeler if the skin is very thick.
2. Plunge the asparagus into a pan of boiling water and cook for 2–3 minutes, or until the asparagus is bright green and just tender. Drain and place on serving plates. Drizzle with a little melted butter. To serve, top the asparagus with shavings of parmesan cheese and sprinkle with cracked black pepper.

You can use green, purple or white asparagus for this recipe, or a combination. Lightly toasted, crushed hazelnuts or pecan nuts can be sprinkled over the top for variation.

Yorkshire Puddings

Serves 8

115 g (4 oz/1 cup) plain (all-purpose) flour
1–2 eggs
250 ml (9 oz/1 cup) milk
1 tablespoon water
3 tablespoons lard or beef dripping, melted

1. Sift the flour and the salt together into a large bowl. Make a well in the centre and add the eggs. Using a wooden spoon, gradually beat in sufficient milk to make a stiff but smooth batter, making sure there are no lumps. Gradually beat in the remaining milk. Strain into a jug. Cover with plastic wrap and refrigerate for 1 hour. Stir in the water.
2. Preheat the oven to 200°C (400°F/Gas 6). Spoon 1/4 teaspoon of the fat into the base of each of 12 deep muffin tins. Place the tins in the hot oven for 3–5 minutes to heat the fat.
3. Carefully fill each Yorkshire pudding tin two-thirds full with batter. Increase the oven temperature to 220°C (425°F/Gas 7).
4. Bake the puddings for 15–20 minutes, or until risen, golden and crisp. Carefully remove the puddings from the tins, transfer to a warm serving dish and serve at once.

You can add 1 tablespoon of chopped fresh herbs or dried thyme to the batter for herbed Yorkshire puddings.

Individual Baked Rösti

Makes 12

500 g (1 lb 2 oz) boiling potatoes, peeled
30 g (1 oz) butter, melted
1 onion

1. Preheat the oven to 220°C (425°F/Gas 7). Cook the potatoes in a pan of boiling salted water for 7 minutes, or until just tender (pierce with the point of a sharp knife—if the knife comes away easily, the potato is ready). Drain and cool.
2. Grease twelve 125 ml (4½ fl oz/½ cup) capacity muffin tins. Grate the potatoes and onion, mix in a bowl and add the butter. Season with salt and mix well. Divide the mixture among the tins, gently pressing in. Bake for 45 minutes, or until the rösti is cooked through and golden brown.
3. With a small palette knife, gently loosen each rösti around the edge and lift out for serving.

Leeks in White Sauce

Serves 6

2 leeks, white part only, trimmed
50 g (1 3/4 oz) butter
1 tablespoon plain (all-purpose) flour
250 ml (9 fl oz/1 cup) milk
2 tablespoons grated cheddar cheese
1 tablespoon dry breadcrumbs

1. Wash the leeks, cut in half lengthways and then into 5 cm (2 inch) pieces. Heat 30 g (1 oz) of the butter in a heavy-based saucepan, add the leeks and cook for 10 minutes, stirring, until tender. Transfer to an ovenproof serving dish.
2. Melt the remaining butter in a pan over low heat. Stir in the flour and cook for 1 minute, or until pale and foaming. Remove from the heat and gradually stir in the milk. Return to the heat and stir until the sauce boils and thickens. Pour over the leeks. Sprinkle with cheese and crumbs. Grill under a preheated grill (broiler) for 2–3 minutes, or until golden brown.

Zucchini with Lemon and Caper Butter

Serves 4

2 tablespoons capers, rinsed and squeezed dry
100 g (3 1/2 oz) butter
2 teaspoons grated lemon zest
1 tablespoon lemon juice
8 small zucchini (courgettes)

1 Chop the capers and put them in a small bowl with the butter, lemon zest, lemon juice and some salt and pepper. Mix until combined. Thinly slice the zucchini lengthways and steam in a saucepan for 3–5 minutes, or until tender. Toss with the caper butter and serve immediately.

Potato and Ham Pancakes

Serves 4–6

500 g (1 lb 2 oz) roasting potatoes
200 g (7 oz) ham slices, finely chopped
4 spring onions (scallions), finely chopped
1 small gherkin, finely chopped
2 tablespoons chopped parsley
1 egg, lightly beaten
50 g (1 3/4 oz) butter

1. Boil or steam the potatoes for 10–15 minutes, until tender (pierce with the point of a small knife—if the potato comes away easily, it is ready). Drain well, then put the potato in a large bowl and mash.
2. Mix in the ham, spring onion, gherkin, parsley, egg and some freshly ground black pepper. Spread on a plate, cover and refrigerate for at least 1 hour, or overnight, to firm.
3. Heat 30 g (1 oz) of the butter in a 20 cm (8 inch) heavy-based frying pan. Add the potato, spread evenly into the pan and smooth the surface with the back of a spoon. Cook over moderate heat for 15 minutes, then slide out onto a plate. Add the remaining butter to the pan, carefully flip the cake back into the pan and cook for another 15–20 minutes, or until the outside forms a brown crust. Cut into wedges for serving.

Potato Croquettes

Makes 12

600 g (1 lb 5 oz) roasting potatoes, peeled and chopped
1 egg
1 egg yolk
60 g (2¼ oz/⅔ cup) parmesan cheese, grated
40 g (1¼ oz/¼ cup) finely chopped ham
3 tablespoons chopped parsley
plain (all-purpose) flour, for coating
1 egg, lightly beaten, extra
100 g (3½ oz/1 cup) dry breadcrumbs
oil, for deep-frying

1. Cook the potato for 5–10 minutes, or until tender (pierce with the point of a small knife—if the potato comes away easily, it is ready). Drain and mash thoroughly. While the potato is still hot, gradually stir or fold in the combined beaten egg and egg yolk, parmesan cheese, ham and parsley. Divide into 12 portions, put on a tray, cover with plastic wrap and refrigerate for at least 1 hour.

2. Shape the potato portions into small sausage shapes and coat each in the flour, egg and then the breadcrumbs. Put the croquettes on a baking tray covered with baking paper. Refrigerate for at least 30 minutes, to firm.

3. Fill a large heavy-based saucepan one third full of oil and heat to 180°C (350°F), or until a cube of bread browns in 15 seconds. Cook the potato croquettes, three or four at a time so the pan does not overcrowd, for 2 minutes, or until evenly browned and heated through. Drain on crumpled paper towels. Serve hot or warm.

Risotto-stuffed Onions

Serves 8

8 large onions
1 tablespoon oil
20 g (3/4 oz) butter
70 g (2 1/2 oz/3/4 cup) chopped button mushrooms
20 g (3/4 oz) prosciutto slices, chopped
110 g (3 3/4 oz/1/2 cup) risotto rice
600 ml (21 fl oz/2 1/2 cups) hot ready-made chicken stock
2 tablespoons grated parmesan cheese
2 tablespoons chopped parsley

1. Preheat the oven to 200°C (400°F/Gas 6). Take off the outer papery skin of the onions. Trim the bases of the onions so they sit flat and cut the tops off, leaving a wide opening. Place in a baking dish, drizzle with the oil and bake for 1–1 1/2 hours, or until golden.

2. Meanwhile, melt the butter in a pan, add the mushrooms and prosciutto and cook for 5 minutes, or until the mushrooms have softened. Add the rice and stir until well coated with the butter. Gradually stir in the hot chicken stock; about 125 ml (4 1/4 fl oz/1/2 cup) at a time, making sure the liquid has been absorbed before adding more. When all the stock has been absorbed, stir in the cheese and parsley.

3. Scoop out the flesh from the middle of each onion, leaving at least 3 outside layers on each, to hold the filling. Chop the scooped flesh and stir through the risotto mixture. Spoon the filling into the onion shells, piling a little on top. Bake for 10 minutes to heat through, then serve.

Coleslaw

Serves 10

1/2 green cabbage

1/4 red cabbage

3 carrots, coarsely grated

6 radishes, coarsely grated

1 red capsicum (pepper), chopped

4 spring onions (scallions), sliced

3 tablespoons chopped flat-leaf (Italian) parsley

250 g (9 oz/1 cup) whole-egg mayonnaise

1. Remove the hard cores from the cabbages and thinly shred the leaves with a sharp knife. Place in a large bowl and add the carrot, radish, capsicum, spring onion and parsley.
2. Add the mayonnaise, season with salt and freshly ground black pepper and toss well.

Cold Potato Salad

Serves 8

1.25 kg (2 lb 12 oz) boiling potatoes, unpeeled
2 onions, finely chopped
2 green capsicums (peppers), chopped
4–5 celery stalks, chopped
2 large handfuls finely chopped parsley

DRESSING
375 g (13 oz/1 1/2 cups) whole-egg mayonnaise
3–4 tablespoons white wine vinegar or lemon juice, to taste
90 g (3 1/4 oz/1/3 cup) sour cream

1. Cut the potatoes into bite-size pieces. Steam or boil the potatoes for 5–10 minutes, or until just tender (pierce with the point of a small sharp knife—if the potato comes away easily it is ready). Don't let the skins break away. Drain and cool completely.
2. Combine the onion, capsicum, celery and parsley with the potato in a large bowl, reserving some parsley for garnish.
3. To make the dressing, mix together all the ingredients in a bowl and season with salt and black pepper. Pour over the salad and toss gently. Garnish with the reserved parsley.

Mushy Peas with Fennel and Spring Onion

Serves 6

320 g (11¼ oz/2 cups) shelled peas
1 small potato
20 g (¾ oz) butter
1 tablespoon oil
1 baby fennel bulb
250 ml (9 fl oz/1 cup) milk
pinch ground nutmeg
4 spring onions (scallions)
1 small handful chopped fennel leaves
extra virgin olive oil, to serve

1. Wash and peel the potato and cut it into 2 cm (¾ inch) cubes. Thinly slice the fennel bulb and spring onions.
2. Heat the butter and oil in a large saucepan, over medium-low heat and fry the fennel for 3–4 minutes, or until soft. Add the peas, potato, milk and enough water to just cover the vegetables. Simmer for about 15 minutes, until the peas and potato are tender and the liquid has evaporated. Stir regularly towards the end of the cooking time to prevent sticking. Season with salt, pepper and nutmeg, to taste. Remove from the heat.
3. Add the spring onions and fennel leaves. Roughly break up the mixture using a potato masher or fork. Serve hot, drizzled with extra virgin olive oil, to taste.

Orange Sweet Potato

Serves 4

800 g (1 lb 12 oz) orange sweet potato
20 g (3/4 oz) butter, melted
2 teaspoons sesame seeds
1/2 teaspoon cracked black pepper

1 Preheat the oven to 180°C (350°F/Gas 4). Cut the sweet potato into 1 cm (1/2 inch) thick slices. Combine with the butter, sesame seeds and pepper. Toss, then roast in a baking dish for 25 minutes, or until lightly browned and tender, turning once. Sprinkle with salt before serving.

Roast Onions

Serves 6

6 onions
60 g (2 1/4 oz/3/4 cup) fresh breadcrumbs
25 g (1 oz/1/4 cup) grated parmesan cheese
1 tablespoon chopped basil
20 g (3/4 oz) butter, melted

1. Preheat the oven to 180°C (350°F/Gas 4). Peel the onions, leaving the root ends intact. Place in a pan of water, bring to the boil and simmer gently for 20 minutes. Remove and cool. Cut off and discard the top quarter of each onion, and scoop out a third of the inside. Combine the breadcrumbs, cheese, basil and butter in a bowl and season. Spoon into the onions and roast in a lightly greased baking dish for 50 minutes, or until the onions are soft.

Brussels Sprouts and Chestnuts

Serves 8

240 g (8½ oz/1½ cups) fresh or tin chestnuts
1 kg (2 lb 4 oz) brussels sprouts
30 g (1 oz) butter
freshly grated nutmeg, to taste

1. If using fresh chestnuts, make slits in the skins of the chestnuts. Put them in a saucepan. Cover with cold water and bring to the boil over high heat. Reduce the heat and simmer for 10 minutes. Drain and leave until cool enough to handle. Peel off the skins.

2. Trim the sprouts and cut a cross in the base of each. Bring a pan of water to the boil, add the sprouts and simmer for 5–8 minutes, or until just tender. Melt the butter in a large frying pan and add the chestnuts. Cook until they begin to brown, then add the sprouts and toss together until heated through. Season well with salt, pepper and nutmeg.

Herbed Carrots

Serves 6

8 carrots
40 g (1 1/2 oz) butter
2 teaspoons sugar
2 teaspoons lemon juice
2 teaspoons finely chopped flat-leaf (Italian) parsley

1. Peel the carrots and cut into thick matchsticks. Cook in a saucepan of boiling water for 3–5 minutes, or until tender. Drain well.
2. Melt the butter in the pan and add the sugar. Return the carrots to the saucepan and toss together until the carrots start to colour a little. Add the lemon juice and parsley and toss together until the carrots are well coated.

Roast Parsnips

Serves 4

4 parsnips, peeled
1 tablespoon oil
20 g (3/4 oz) butter, melted
1 tablespoon golden (dark corn) syrup

1 Preheat the oven to 180°C (350°F/Gas 4). Cut off the thin part of the parsnips, then cut each thick section into quarters lengthways. Toss with the oil and butter in a baking dish and roast for 35 minutes, or until lightly browned, tossing occasionally. Drizzle with golden syrup and roast for a further 5 minutes.

Roast Pumpkin

Serves 4–6

1 kg (2 lb 4 oz) pumpkin (winter squash)
1 tablespoon oil
20 g (3/4 oz) butter, melted
1/2 teaspoon ground paprika
1/2 teaspoon ground cumin

1 Preheat the oven to 180°C (350°F/Gas 4). Cut the pumpkin into 8 pieces and toss with the oil, butter, paprika and cumin. Roast in a baking dish for 40 minutes, or until brown and tender, turning once. Serve hot.

Stuffed Tomatoes

Serves 6

6 ripe tomatoes
20 g (3/4 oz) butter
2 bacon slices, finely chopped
75 g (2 1/2 oz/3/4 cup) finely chopped button mushrooms
1 spring onion (scallion), finely chopped
80 g (2 3/4 oz/1 cup) fresh breadcrumbs
oil, for drizzling

1. Preheat the oven to 180°C (350°F/Gas 4). Cut the tops off the tomatoes, reserving the tops. Scoop out the seeds and soft flesh. In a frying pan, melt the butter over low heat and fry the bacon and button mushrooms for 5 minutes, or until soft. Transfer to a bowl.

2. Stir in the spring onion and breadcrumbs and season with salt and freshly ground black pepper. Fill the tomatoes with the mixture and replace the tops. Place on a baking tray and drizzle with oil. Roast for 20 minutes, or until heated through.

Braised Fennel

Serves 8

4 small fennel bulbs
20 g (3/4 oz) butter
1 tablespoon sugar
80 ml (2 1/2 fl oz/1/3 cup) white wine
160 ml (5 1/4 fl oz/2/3 cup) ready-made chicken stock
1 tablespoon sour cream

1. Slice the fennel bulbs into quarters, reserving the fronds. Melt the butter in a frying pan and stir in the sugar. Add the fennel, and cook for 5–10 minutes, until lightly browned all over.
2. Pour in the wine and stock and bring to the boil, then reduce the heat and simmer, covered, for 10 minutes, or until tender.
3. Uncover and boil until most of the liquid has evaporated and the sauce has become sticky. Remove from the heat and stir in the sour cream. Garnish with the reserved fennel fronds.

Broccoli with Almonds

Serves 6

500 g (1 lb 2 oz) broccoli, cut into small florets
2 teaspoons oil
20 g (3/4 oz) butter
1 garlic clove, crushed
1 tablespoon flaked almonds

1. Add the broccoli to a saucepan of boiling water and cook for 1–2 minutes, or until just tender. Drain thoroughly. Heat the oil and butter in a large frying pan, add the garlic and almonds and cook for 1–2 minutes, or until the almonds are golden. Remove from the pan and set aside.
2. Add the broccoli to the frying pan and toss over medium heat for 2–3 minutes, or until the broccoli is heated through. Return the almonds to the pan and stir until well distributed. Serve hot.

Celeriac and Tarragon Purée

Serves 6

500 ml (17 fl oz/2 cups) ready-made vegetable stock
60 ml (2 fl oz/1/4 cup) lemon juice
3 celeriac, peeled and chopped
40 g (1 1/2 oz) butter
1 tablespoon cream (whipping)
1 tablespoon finely chopped tarragon

1. Put the vegetable stock, lemon juice and 500 ml (17 fl oz/2 cups) water in a saucepan and bring to the boil. Add the celeriac and cook for 10–15 minutes, or until tender. You may need to add extra water, depending on the size of the celeriac.
2. Drain, and place celeriac in a food processor with the butter and cream. Season with salt and freshly ground pepper and process until smooth. Alternatively, you can mash until smooth. Stir in the chopped tarragon. If the mixture is too thick, add a little more cream.

Minted Peas

Serves 6

625 g (1 lb 6 oz/4 cups) peas, fresh or frozen
4 sprigs mint
30 g (1 oz) butter
2 tablespoons shredded mint leaves

1. Place the peas in a saucepan and pour in water to just cover the peas. Add the mint sprigs.
2. Bring to the boil and simmer for 5 minutes (only 2 minutes if frozen), or until the peas are just tender. Drain and discard the mint. Return to the saucepan, add the butter and shredded mint and stir over low heat until the butter has melted. Season with salt and cracked pepper.

Honeyed Turnips with Lemon Thyme

Serves 4

500 g (1 lb 2 oz) baby turnips
40 g (1 1/2 oz) butter
4 tablespoons clear honey
1 tablespoon lemon juice
1/2 teaspoon grated lemon zest
1 tablespoon lemon thyme leaves

1. Rinse and lightly scrub the turnips under cold running water. Trim the tips and stalks. Cook in boiling water for 1 minute. Drain, rinse under cold water and drain again.
2. Heat the butter in a saucepan. Add the honey and bring to the boil, then add the lemon juice and zest. Continue to boil over a high heat for 3 minutes. Add the turnips to the pan. Cook over high heat for a further 3 minutes, or until the turnips are almost tender and well glazed (test with a skewer).
3. Add the lemon thyme. Remove the pan from the heat and toss until the turnips are well coated with the honey and thyme mixture. Serve warm.

Game Chips

Serves 4

500 g (1 lb 2 oz) old potatoes
vegetable oil, for deep-frying

1. Peel and slice the potatoes very thinly, using a sharp knife. Put the slices in a bowl, cover with cold water and set aside for 1 hour. Drain and dry thoroughly on paper towels.
2. Heat the oil for deep-frying in a heavy-based frying pan to 180°C (350°F) or until a cube of bread browns in 30 seconds. Fry the potatoes in small batches until light golden brown. Remove from the pan and drain well on paper towels.
3. To serve, reheat the oil and fry the potatoes again until they are crisp. Drain and serve immediately with roast game, turkey or goose.

Chickpea and Roast Vegetable Salad

Serves 8

500 g (1 lb 2 oz) butternut pumpkin (squash), cut into chunks
2 red capsicums (peppers), halved
4 slender eggplants (aubergines), sliced in half lengthways
4 zucchini (courgettes), sliced in half lengthways
4 onions, quartered
olive oil, for brushing
600 g (1 lb 5 oz/2 3/4 cups) tin chickpeas, rinsed and drained
2 tablespoons chopped flat-leaf (Italian) parsley

DRESSING
80 ml (2 1/2 fl oz/1/3 cup) olive oil
2 tablespoons lemon juice
1 garlic clove, crushed
1 tablespoon chopped thyme

1. Preheat the oven to 220°C (425°F/Gas 7). Grease two baking trays and spread the vegetables in a single layer over the trays. Brush the vegetables lightly with the olive oil.
2. Bake for 40 minutes, or until the vegetables are tender and begin to brown slightly on the edges. Remove and set aside to cool. Remove the skins from the capsicums if you wish. Chop the capsicum, eggplant and zucchini into large pieces, then put all the vegetables in a bowl with the chickpeas and half the parsley.
3. To make the dressing, whisk together all the dressing ingredients in a bowl. Season, then toss through the vegetables. Set aside for 30 minutes to marinate. Spoon into a serving bowl and sprinkle with the rest of the parsley before serving.

Creamy Potato Gratin

Serves 6

750 g (1 lb 10 oz) boiling potatoes
1 onion
125 g (4 1/2 oz/1 cup) grated cheddar cheese
375 ml (13 fl oz/1 1/2 cups) cream (whipping)
2 teaspoons chicken stock (bouillon) powder

1. Preheat the oven to 180°C (350°F/Gas 4). Thinly slice the potatoes and slice the onion into rings.
2. Arrange a layer of overlapping potato slices in a baking dish and top with a layer of onion rings. Divide the cheese in half and set aside one half for the topping. Sprinkle a little of the remaining cheese over the onion. Continue layering in this order until all the potato and the onion have been used, finishing with a little cheese.
3. Pour the cream into a small jug, add the chicken stock powder and whisk gently until thoroughly combined. Pour the mixture over the layered potato and onion and sprinkle the top with the reserved cheese. Bake for 40 minutes, or until the potato is tender, the cheese has melted and the top is golden brown.

Sweet Roast Beetroot

Serves 6

12 small fresh beetroot (beets)
$1^1/2$ tablespoons olive oil
20 g ($^3/4$ oz) butter
$1^1/2$ teaspoons ground cumin
1 teaspoon coriander seeds, lightly crushed
$^1/2$ teaspoon mixed (pumpkin pie) spice
1 garlic clove, crushed, optional
3–4 teaspoons soft brown sugar
1 tablespoon balsamic vinegar

1 Preheat the oven to 180°C (350°F/Gas 4). Grease a baking tray. Trim the leafy tops from the beetroot (cut about 3 cm/$1^1/4$ inches above the bulb to prevent bleeding), wash the bulbs thoroughly and place on the tray. Bake for $1^1/4$ hours or until very tender. Set aside until the bulbs are cool enough to handle.

2 Peel the beetroot and trim the tops and tails to neaten. Heat the oil and butter in a frying pan, add the cumin, coriander seeds, mixed spice and garlic and cook over medium heat for 1 minute. Add the sugar and vinegar to the pan and stir for 2–3 minutes, or until the sugar dissolves. Add the beetroot, reduce the heat to low and turn the beetroot for 5 minutes, or until glazed all over. Serve warm or at room temperature.

Spiced Red Cabbage

Serves 6

750 g (1 lb 10 oz) red cabbage
1 large red onion, chopped
1 green apple, cored and chopped
2 garlic cloves, crushed
1/4 teaspoon ground cloves
1/4 teaspoon ground nutmeg
1 1/2 tablespoons soft brown sugar
2 tablespoons red wine vinegar
20 g (3/4 oz) butter, chilled and cubed

1. Preheat the oven to 150°C (300°F/Gas 2). Quarter the cabbage and remove the core. Finely slice the cabbage and put it in a large baking dish with the onion and apple. Toss well.

2. Combine the garlic, spices, sugar and vinegar in a small bowl. Pour the mixture over the cabbage, and toss. Dot the top with the butter. Cover and bake for 1 1/2 hours, stirring once or twice. Season with salt and freshly ground black pepper, to taste, and serve hot.

Cauliflower Cheese

Serves 4

500 g (1 lb 2 oz) cauliflower, cut into small pieces
2 tablespoons fresh breadcrumbs
30 g (1 oz/1/4 cup) grated cheddar cheese

CHEESE SAUCE
30 g (1 oz) butter
30 g (1 oz/1/4 cup) plain (all-purpose) flour
315 ml (10 3/4 fl oz/1 1/4 cups) warm milk
1 teaspoon dijon mustard
60 g (2 1/4 oz/1/2 cup) grated cheddar cheese
50 g (1 3/4 oz/1/2 cup) grated parmesan cheese

1. Lightly grease a 1.5 litre (52 fl oz) heatproof dish. Cook the small cauliflower pieces in a saucepan of lightly salted boiling water for 10 minutes, or until just tender. Drain thoroughly, then transfer to the prepared dish and keep warm.

2. To make the cheese sauce, melt the butter in a pan over low heat. Stir in the flour and cook for 1 minute, or until pale and foaming. Remove from the heat and gradually stir in the milk and mustard. Return to the heat and stir constantly until the sauce boils and thickens. Reduce the heat and simmer for 2 minutes, then remove from the heat. Add the cheddar and parmesan cheese and stir until melted. Do not reheat or the oil will come out of the cheese. Season with salt and white pepper, to taste, and pour over the cauliflower.

3. Combine the breadcrumbs and cheddar cheese and sprinkle over the sauce. Grill (broil) under medium heat until the top is brown and bubbling. Serve immediately.

Beans with Artichokes and Olives

Serves 4

200 g (7 oz) baby beans
8 spring onions (scallions)
1 tablespoon olive oil
6 rosemary sprigs
85 g (3 oz/1/2 cup) green olives
2 artichoke hearts, quartered
1 tablespoon capers, rinsed and squeezed dry
1 tablespoon extra virgin olive oil
2 teaspoons tarragon vinegar (see page 138)

1. Blanch the baby beans in boiling salted water for 2 minutes, then drain. Trim the spring onions to roughly the same length as the beans.
2. Heat the olive oil in a large frying pan over medium heat. Sauté the beans, spring onions and rosemary for 1–2 minutes, or until lightly browned. Remove from the heat. Add the green olives, artichokes, capers, olive oil and vinegar. Season with salt and pepper and toss to coat the vegetables with the oil and vinegar. Pile in a dish and serve warm or at room temperature.

Eggnog Custard Roast Turkey Pudding Tr

Sauces and stuffings
Cranberry Sauce Orange Glazed Ham

Apple Sauce

4 green apples
1 tablespoon caster (superfine) sugar
2 cloves, whole
1 cinnamon stick
2 teaspoons lemon juice

1. Peel and core the apples, then roughly chop the flesh. Put the flesh in a pan with the caster sugar and 125 ml (4 1/2 fl oz/1/2 cup) water. Add the cloves and the cinnamon stick. Cover and simmer for 10 minutes, or until soft. Remove from the heat and discard the cloves and cinnamon stick. Mash or, for a finer sauce, press through a sieve. Stir in the lemon juice to taste.

Serve with roast pork or ham.

Honey Mustard Sauce

250 ml (9 fl oz/1 cup) white wine
1 tablespoon dijon mustard
60 g (2 1/4 oz/1/4 cup) wholegrain mustard
2 tablespoons honey
200 g (7 oz) chilled butter, cubed

1. Pour the wine into a saucepan and cook over high heat for 5 minutes, or until reduced by half. Add the mustards and honey. Reduce the heat to a simmer and slowly whisk in the butter, without boiling. Remove from the heat and season, to taste, before serving.

Serve with beef, ham or veal.

Dill Mayonnaise

1 egg, at room temperature
1 egg yolk, at room temperature
1 tablespoon lemon juice
1 teaspoon white wine vinegar
375 ml (13 fl oz/1 1/2 cups) light olive oil
1–2 tablespoons chopped dill

1 Combine the egg, yolk, lemon juice and wine vinegar until blended. Add the oil in a thin, steady stream, stirring constantly until all the oil is added and the mayonnaise is thick and creamy—it should be thick enough to form peaks. Transfer to a bowl and stir in the dill and salt and pepper, to taste.

Serve with poached or steamed fish. Also goes well with vegetables.

Mint Sauce

3 tablespoons caster (superfine) sugar
1 large handful mint leaves
60 ml (2 fl oz/1/4 cup) boiling water
185 ml (6 fl oz/3/4 cup) malt vinegar

1. Sprinkle 1 tablespoon of the caster sugar over the mint leaves on a chopping board, then finely chop the mint. Transfer the leaves to a bowl and add the rest of the caster sugar. Cover with the boiling water and stir until the sugar has dissolved. Stir in the malt vinegar, cover and chill overnight.

Traditionally mint sauce is served with roast lamb.

Horseradish Cream

175 g (6 oz/2 cups) freshly grated or bottled horseradish cream
1 spring onion (scallion), finely chopped
60 g (2 1/4 oz/1/4 cup) sour cream
125 ml (4 fl oz/1/2 cup) cream (whipping), whipped

1 Combine the horseradish cream, spring onion and sour cream in a bowl. Fold in the whipped cream. Season.

Serve with poached or steamed fish, smoked salmon, roast beef or veal.

Bread Sauce

1 onion

4 whole cloves

750 ml (26 fl oz/3 cups) milk

2 bay leaves

150 g (5$^1/_2$ oz/2 cups) fresh breadcrumbs

25 g (1 oz) butter

1. Peel the onion and stud it with the cloves. Place the onion in a saucepan with the milk and bay leaves. Bring to the boil, remove from the heat and cover. Leave the mixture for 30 minutes so the flavours infuse. Remove and discard the onion and bay leaves.
2. Add the breadcrumbs and bring to the boil, stirring constantly. Lower the heat and simmer for 3–4 minutes. Stir in the butter and season with salt and pepper, to taste.

Serve warm with roast chicken, turkey, goose or game meat.

Tarragon Mayonnaise

2 egg yolks
1 teaspoon dijon mustard
4 teaspoons lemon juice
250 ml (9 fl oz/1 cup) light olive oil
2 teaspoons chopped French tarragon

1. Place the egg yolks, dijon mustard and 2 teaspoons of lemon juice in a food processor and process for 10 seconds. With the motor running, add the olive oil in a slow, thin stream until combined. Stir in the other 2 teaspoons of lemon juice and the tarragon, and season with salt and white pepper, to taste.

Serve with steamed fish or vegetables.

Beetroot Relish

750 g (1 lb 10 oz/5 1/3 cups) grated fresh beetroot (beets)
1 onion, chopped
400 g (14 oz) green apples, peeled, cored and chopped
420 ml (14 1/2 fl oz/1 2/3 cups) white wine vinegar
95 g (3 1/4 oz/1/2 cup) soft brown sugar
110 g (3 3/4 oz/1/2 cup) sugar
2 tablespoons lemon juice
2 teaspoons salt

1. Put the beetroot in a large saucepan with the onion, green apples, white wine vinegar, soft brown sugar, sugar, lemon juice and salt and stir over low heat, without boiling, until all the sugar has dissolved. Bring to the boil and simmer, stirring often, for 20–30 minutes, or until the beetroot and onion are tender and the relish is reduced and thickened.

2. Spoon into clean, warm jars and seal. Turn the jars upside down for 2 minutes, invert and leave to cool. Label and date each jar. Leave for a month before using. Store in a cool, dark place for up to 12 months. Refrigerate after opening, for up to 6 weeks.

Serve with ham, beef, turkey, duck or goose.

Orange and Cranberry Sauce

250 ml (9 fl oz/1 cup) white wine
250 ml (9 fl oz/1 cup) ready-made chicken stock
280 g (10 oz/1 cup) cranberry sauce
2 strips orange zest, white pith removed
1 tablespoon cornflour (cornstarch)

1 Mix together the white wine, chicken stock and cranberry sauce in a saucepan. Add the orange zest and stir until the cranberry sauce has dissolved. Bring to the boil, reduce the heat slightly and simmer for 5 minutes. Stir the cornflour with a little water to make a smooth paste. Add the paste to the pan and stir until the mixture boils and thickens, then simmer for a further 2 minutes. Remove and discard the orange zest before serving.

Serve with roast turkey, veal, ham or duck.

Fruit Chutney

400 g (14 oz) chopped onions
250 g (9 oz) green apples, cored and peeled
4 garlic cloves, finely chopped
1 teaspoon ground cumin
1 teaspoon ground coriander
1 teaspoon ground cloves
1 teaspoon ground cayenne pepper
600 g (1 lb 5 oz/3 1/4 cups) soft brown sugar, lightly packed
600 ml (21 fl oz/2 1/3 cups) malt vinegar

1. Finely chop the apricots, peaches, pears, raisins, dates and apples. Place in a large saucepan with the onion. Add the garlic, cumin, coriander, cloves, cayenne pepper, sugar and vinegar. Add 2 teaspoons of salt and 750 ml (26 fl oz/3 cups) water to the pan. Stir over a low heat until all the sugar has dissolved.
2. Increase the heat and bring to the boil, then reduce the heat and simmer, stirring often, over medium heat for 1 1/2 hours, or until the mixture has thickened and the fruit is soft and pulpy. Do not cook over high heat because the liquid will evaporate too quickly and the flavours will not have time to fully develop.
3. Spoon the mixture immediately into clean, warm jars and seal. Turn upside-down for 2 minutes, then invert and leave to cool. Label and date each jar. Leave for 1 month before opening to allow the flavours to develop. Store in a cool, dark place for up to 12 months.

Serve with cold meats. Refrigerate after opening.

Tarragon Vinegar

500 ml (17 fl oz/2 cups) white wine vinegar
1 large handful fresh tarragon leaves
tarragon sprig, to taste

1 Warm the vinegar in a saucepan over low heat. Gently bruise the tarragon leaves and put them in a 500 ml (17 fl oz/2 cup) glass bottle. Pour in the vinegar, seal with a non-metallic lid and shake well. Leave to infuse in a warm place for about 2 weeks. Strain and return to the clean, warm sterilized bottle. Add a a sprig of tarragon, then seal, label and date. Store in a cold dark place until needed.

Use as a flavoured vinaigrette for beans with artichokes and olives (see page 125).

Classic Gravy

2 tablespoons roast meat juice, drained

1 tablespoon brandy

2 tablespoons plain (all-purpose) flour

375 ml (13 fl oz/1 1/2 cups) ready-made chicken or beef stock

1 Drain off all but 2 tablespoons of the juices left in the baking tin of the roasted meat. Place the baking dish on top of the stove over medium heat, add the brandy and stir quickly to lift the sticky juices from the bottom of the pan. Cook for 1 minute. Remove from the heat, stir in the flour and mix well. Return the pan to the heat and cook for 2 minutes, stirring constantly. Remove from the heat and gradually stir in the stock. Return to the heat and cook, stirring constantly, until the gravy boils and thickens. Season to taste, with salt and pepper.

Serve with roast beef, lamb, chicken, pork, roast potatoes and Yorkshire puddings.

Rice and Fruit Stuffing

280 g (10 oz/1 1/2 cups) cooked long-grain white rice
40 g (1 1/2 oz/1/4 cup) pine nuts
180 g (6 oz/1 cup) dried apricots, chopped
220 g (7 3/4 oz/1 cup) chopped pitted prunes
4 spring onions (scallions), sliced
1 tablespoon finely grated orange zest
80 ml (2 1/2 fl oz/1/3 cup) orange juice
1 egg, lightly beaten

1. Preheat the oven to 180°C (350°F/Gas 4). Spread the pine nuts on a baking tray and bake for 5 minutes, or until lightly golden. Watch carefully as they will burn easily.
2. Combine the rice, pine nuts, apricots, prunes, spring onion, orange zest, juice, 1/2 teaspoon salt and some white pepper. Mix well and stir in the egg.

Excellent with roast turkey and turkey buffe.

Citrus Stuffing

1 tablespoon oil, for frying
1 onion, finely chopped
200 g (7 oz) minced (ground) sausage
2 garlic cloves, crushed
160 g (5 3/4 oz/2 cups) fresh breadcrumbs
2 teaspoons grated lemon zest
2 teaspoons grated orange zest
60 g (2 1/4 oz/1/2 cup) chopped pecans

1. Heat the oil in a small frying pan and cook the onion until soft. Transfer to a large bowl and cool. Add the sausage mince, garlic, breadcrumbs, lemon and orange zest and pecans and mix well. Season, to taste, with salt and pepper.

Excellent with roast chicken and turkey.

Country Sage Stuffing

45 g ($1^1/_2$ oz) butter
1 onion, finely chopped
1 celery stalk, sliced
10 sage leaves, torn
160 g ($5^3/_4$ oz/2 cups) fresh breadcrumbs
$1^1/_2$ teaspoons dried sage
4 tablespoons chopped parsley
2 egg whites, lightly beaten

1 Melt the butter in a small saucepan and cook the onion and celery over medium heat for 3 minutes, or until the onion has softened. Transfer to a bowl and add the sage leaves, breadcrumbs, dried sage, parsley, egg whites, 1 teaspoon salt and $^1/_2$ teaspoon white pepper. Mix until well combined.

Excellent with roast chicken and turkey.

Cashew Nut Stuffing

60 g ($2^{1}/_{4}$ oz) butter
1 onion, chopped
370 g (13 oz/2 cups) cooked long-grain brown rice
185 g ($6^{1}/_{2}$ oz/1 cup) dried apricots, chopped
80 g ($2^{3}/_{4}$ oz/$^{1}/_{2}$ cup) unsalted cashew nuts
3 tablespoons chopped parsley
2 tablespoons chopped mint
1 tablespoon lemon juice

1 Melt the butter in a frying pan and cook the onion until golden. Cool, then mix thoroughly with the cooked long-grain brown rice, dried apricots, cashew nuts, parsley, mint and lemon juice. Season, to taste, with salt and pepper.

Excellent with roast chicken and turkey.

Spinach and Ricotta Stuffing

2 tablespoons oil
1 onion, finely chopped
2 garlic cloves, crushed
500 g (1 lb 2 oz) frozen English spinach, thawed
80 g (2 3/4 oz/3/4 cup) pine nuts
80 g dry (2 3/4 oz/3/4 cup) fresh breadcrumbs
400 g (14 oz/1 2/3 cups) ricotta cheese
200 g (7 oz/1 1/3 cups) semi-dried tomatoes, finely chopped

1. Heat the oil in a small saucepan, add the onion and garlic and cook, stirring over medium heat for 5 minutes, or until soft. Squeeze as much liquid as possible from the thawed spinach and add the spinach to the pan. Cook, stirring for 2–3 minutes, or until as dry as possible. Remove from the heat and place in a large bowl to cool. Add the pine nuts, breadcrumbs, ricotta and semi-dried tomatoes. Season, to taste, with salt and pepper.

Excellent with roast chicken and turkey.

Breadcrumb Stuffing

3 bacon slices, finely chopped
6 slices wholemeal (whole-wheat) bread
3 spring onions (scallions), chopped
2 tablespoons chopped pecans
2 teaspoons currants
4 tablespoons finely chopped parsley
1 egg, lightly beaten
4 tablespoons milk

1. Dry-fry the bacon in a small frying pan over a high heat for 5 minutes, or until crisp. Remove the crusts from the bread and discard. Cut the bread into 1 cm (1/2 inch) cubes and place in a large mixing bowl. Add the bacon, spring onions, nuts, currants and parsley. In a separate bowl mix together the egg and the milk. Add to the stuffing mixture, season and mix well.

Excellent with roast chicken and turkey.

Spicy Chicken Stuffing

2 teaspoons olive oil
6 spring onions (scallions), finely chopped
500 g (1 lb 2 oz) minced (ground) chicken
80 g (2 3/4 oz/1 cup) fresh breadcrumbs
1 teaspoon grated fresh ginger
2 red chillies, seeded and chopped
2 eggs, lightly beaten
40 g (1 1/2 oz/1/3 cup) chopped pecans
1/2 teaspoon ground black pepper
1/4 teaspoon paprika
1/2 teaspoon ground coriander

1. Heat the oil in a large heavy-based frying pan. Add the onion and chicken mince and cook over medium heat for 4 minutes, or until brown. Use a fork to break up any lumps. Remove from the heat and add the remaining stuffing ingredients. Stir to combine until the mixture is fairly smooth.

Excellent with baked veal.

Sage and Onion Stuffing

25 g (1 oz) butter
1 large onion, finely chopped
2 bacon slices, chopped
1 tablespoon chopped sage
2 teaspoons grated lemon zest
175 g (6 oz/1¾ cups) dry breadcrumbs
1 egg, lightly beaten

1. Heat the butter in a saucepan. Add the onion and bacon and cook, stirring constantly, until soft. Mix together the onion and bacon mixture with the sage, lemon zest, breadcrumbs and egg.

Excellent with roast chicken and turkey.

Orange and Rosemary Stuffing

50 g ($1^3/_4$ oz/$^2/_3$ cup) fresh breadcrumbs
2 tablespoons finely chopped rosemary
2 tablespoons chopped pecans
1 tablespoon orange marmalade
2 teaspoons grated orange zest
2 tablespoons orange juice

1 Mix together the breadcrumbs, rosemary and pecans. Mix together the marmalade, orange zest and the orange juice and add to the breadcrumb mixture. Mix lightly, adding extra orange juice as necessary.

Excellent with roast chicken and turkey.

Pistachio Nut Stuffing

1 tablespoon oil
3 spring onions (scallions), finely chopped
1 teaspoon grated ginger
3 bacon slices, chopped
175 g (6 oz) minced (ground) pork and veal
50 g (1 3/4 oz/2/3 cup) fresh breadcrumbs
3 tablespoons orange marmalade
4 tablespoons chopped parsley
1 egg, lightly beaten
50 g (1 3/4 oz/1/3 cup) pistachio nuts

1 Heat the oil in a small frying pan and cook the spring onions and ginger for 2 minutes. Add the bacon and cook for a further 3–4 minutes. Transfer to a bowl to cool. When cool, add the pork and veal mince, breadcrumbs, marmalade, parsley, egg and pistachio nuts, and season with salt and pepper to taste. Mix well.

Excellent with roast chicken and turkey.

Rice Stuffing

25 g (1 oz/$^{1}/_{4}$ cup) flaked almonds
50 g ($1^{3}/_{4}$ oz) butter
1 onion, finely chopped
1 apple, cored, peeled and grated
4 tablespoons drained and chopped water chestnuts
2 tablespoons chopped parsley
1 egg, lightly beaten
225 g (8 oz/$1^{1}/_{4}$ cups) cooked short-grain white rice

1 Lightly toast the flaked almonds in a dry pan until golden, then set aside. Melt the butter in a small saucepan. Add the onion and cook until softened. Mix together the almonds and onions in a bowl. Add the grated apple, water chestnuts, parsley, egg and cooked rice. Season to taste with salt and pepper and mix well.

Excellent with roast chicken and turkey.

Walnut and Ham Stuffing

175 g (6 oz) ham slices, finely chopped
50 g ($1^{3}/_{4}$ oz/$^{1}/_{2}$ cup) walnuts, finely chopped
50 g ($1^{3}/_{4}$ oz/$^{1}/_{2}$ cup) sliced button mushrooms
115 g (4 oz/$1^{1}/_{2}$ cups) fresh breadcrumbs
4 tablespoons chopped parsley
1 egg, lightly beaten

1. Place all the ingredients in a bowl and combine thoroughly.
2. If making the stuffing in advance, place the stuffing in a freezer container or plastic bag. Seal and freeze until required. Thaw completely before using.

Excellent with roast chicken and turkey.

Créme Anglaise

3 egg yolks
2 tablespoons caster (superfine) sugar
375 ml (13 fl oz/1 1/2 cups) milk
1/2 teaspoon natural vanilla extract

1. Whisk the egg yolks and caster sugar together in a heatproof bowl for 2 minutes, or until light and creamy.
2. Heat the milk in a saucepan until almost boiling, then pour into the bowl, whisking constantly. Return to the clean saucepan and stir over low heat for 5 minutes, or until thick enough to coat the back of a spoon. Don't let the mixture boil or it will curdle. Remove from the heat. Stir in the vanilla. Transfer to a jug to serve.

Serve with cakes, tarts, puddings and stewed fruits.

Rum and Raisin Caramel Sauce

2 1/2 tablespoons chopped raisins
80 ml (2 1/2 fl oz/1/3 cup) rum
230 g (8 oz/1 cup) caster (superfine) sugar
125 ml (4 fl oz/1/2 cup) cream (whipping)
1 teaspoon natural vanilla extract

1. Combine the raisins and rum in a small bowl, cover with plastic wrap and leave to stand for 2 hours.
2. Put the caster sugar and 125 ml (4 fl oz/1/2 cup) water in a small saucepan, stirring to dissolve the sugar. Then, without stirring, bring slowly to a boil.
3. Cook the mixture over medium heat for 12–13 minutes, or until the liquid turns a deep caramel colour. Working quickly, remove the caramel from the heat, add the raisin mixture and the cream, taking care as the caramel is very hot and the mixture will spit. Swirl the pan to combine well, stirring a little if needed, then cool slightly. Stir in the vanilla.

Serve the sauce warm or at room temperature with stewed fruits.

Whisky Sauce

2 tablespoons butter
40 g (1 1/2 oz/1/3 cup) plain (all-purpose) flour
500 ml (17 fl oz/2 cups) milk
2 tablespoons caster (superfine) sugar
80 ml (2 1/2 fl oz/1/3 cup) whisky
2 teaspoons butter, extra
1 tablespoon thick (double/heavy) cream

1. Melt the butter in a saucepan over low heat. Remove from the heat and add the plain flour, stirring until combined. Gradually whisk in the milk and caster sugar. Return to medium heat. Stir until the sauce boils and thickens.
2. Reduce the heat and simmer for 10 minutes, stirring occasionally. Remove from the heat and stir in the whisky, the extra butter and the cream. Cover with plastic wrap until ready to serve.

Delicious served with hot puddings.

Grand Marnier Whipped Butter

zest of 1 orange, cut into thin strips
2 tablespoons caster (superfine) sugar
250 g (9 oz) unsalted butter, softened
40 g (1 1/2 oz/1/3 cup) icing (confectioners') sugar
60 ml (2 fl oz/1/4 cup) orange juice
2–3 tablespoons Grand Marnier

1. Put the orange zest into a small saucepan of cold water and bring to the boil. Drain the zest strips and repeat. Return to the zest to the pan with 80 ml (2 1/2 fl oz/1/3 cup) water and the caster sugar. Stir over low heat until the sugar has dissolved, then boil for 2 minutes until thick and syrupy.
2. Beat the butter in a bowl with an electric beater until light and fluffy. Beat in the icing sugar, orange juice and Grand Marnier, to taste, then fold in the orange zest syrup. Don't add the liquid too quickly or the mixture may split. If this happens, beat in enough icing sugar to bring the mixture back together.

Serve a dollop on top of hot puddings.

Brandy Butter

250 g (9 oz) unsalted butter, softened
185 g (6 1/2 oz/1 1/2 cups) icing (confectioners') sugar, sifted
60 ml (2 fl oz/1/4 cup) brandy

1 Cream the butter and icing sugar until smooth and creamy. Gradually add the brandy, beating thoroughly. Refrigerate until required.

Serve a dollop on top of hot puddings.

Dark Chocolate Sauce

150 g ($5^{1}/_{2}$ oz/1 cup) chopped dark chocolate
315 ml ($10^{3}/_{4}$ oz/$1^{1}/_{4}$ cups) cream (whipping)
2 tablespoons caster (superfine) sugar
1 tablespoon liqueur

1 Put the chocolate in a bowl. Bring the cream to the boil in a saucepan. Stir in the caster sugar, then pour it over the chocolate. Leave for 2 minutes, then stir until smooth. Add a spoonful of any liqueur.

Serve warm with profiteroles (see page 190), cakes or ice cream.

Pouring Vanilla Custard

3 egg yolks
2 tablespoons caster (superfine) sugar
375 ml (13 fl oz/1½ cups) milk
1 vanilla bean, split, or 2 teaspoons natural vanilla extract

1. Beat the egg yolks and sugar in a bowl with a balloon whisk until light and fluffy. When properly beaten, the mixture will fall in a ribbon which will hold its shape for a few seconds. Pour the milk into a saucepan and bring to scalding point—small bubbles will appear around the edge. If using a vanilla bean, add it now and leave to infuse for 5–30 minutes, depending on the strength of the flavour required. Stir if a skin appears to be forming.
2. Pour the milk into the egg mixture, stirring with the balloon whisk until well combined. Pour the custard into a metal bowl set over a pan of simmering water and stir over low heat. Keep the custard below simmering point as the egg yolks will thicken evenly if heated slowly. To prevent lumps forming stir continuously.
3. The custard is ready when it forms a coating on the back of the spoon that you can draw a line through which will hold its shape. If using vanilla extract add 2 teaspoons to the finished custard. When ready, either pour it through a sieve into a bowl or plunge the base of the saucepan into cold water to stop the cooking process.
4. If chilling the custard, lay a piece of plastic wrap directly over the surface to prevent a skin from forming.

Serve with sweet pies, pastries, puddings, fruits or jelly.

Coffee Cream Sauce

55 g (2 oz/$^{1}/_{4}$ cup) caster (superfine) sugar
90 g (3$^{1}/_{4}$ oz/$^{1}/_{2}$ cup) soft brown sugar
250 ml (9 fl oz/1 cup) cream (whipping)
1$^{1}/_{2}$ tablespoons instant coffee powder
2 tablespoons Tia Maria or other coffee liqueur, optional

1. Put the caster sugar, brown sugar, cream and coffee powder in a small saucepan. Stir over medium heat, without boiling, until the sugars have completely dissolved.
2. Bring to the boil, then reduce the heat and simmer for 3 minutes, or until the mixture has thickened slightly. Stir in the liqueur, if using. Serve warm over hot puddings.

Serve with steamed puddings.

Eggnog Custard Roast Turkey Pudding Tr

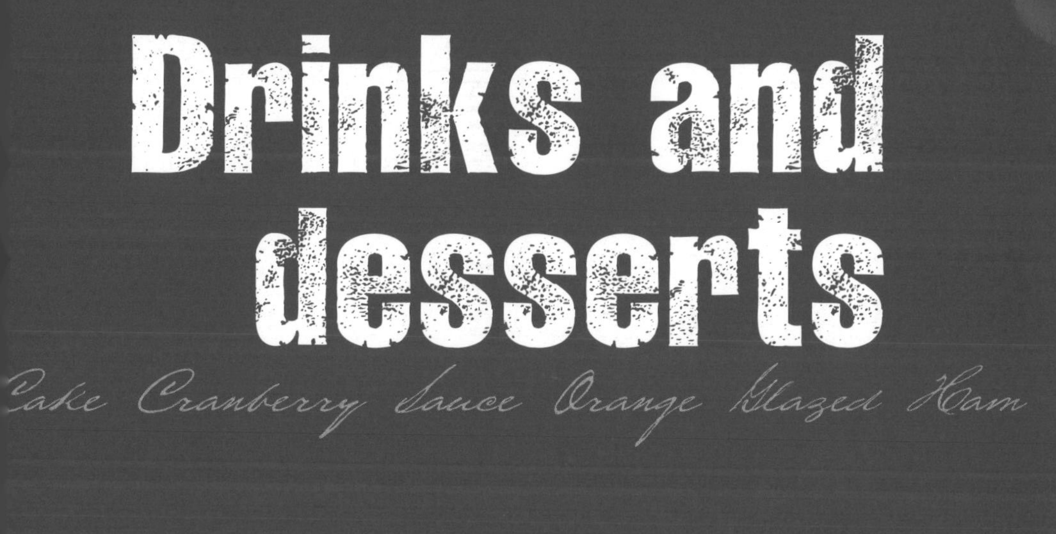
Drinks and desserts
Cranberry Sauce Orange Glazed Ham

Eggnog

Serves 6–8

4 eggs
90 g caster (superfine) sugar
315 ml (10 3/4 fl oz/1 1/4 cups) hot milk
125 ml (4 fl oz/1/2 cup) bourbon
125 ml (4 fl oz/1/2 cup) cream (whipping)
nutmeg, grated, to dust

1. Separate the eggs and set the whites aside. Beat the yolks and the caster sugar in a heatproof bowl until light and fluffy. Add the hot milk and stir to combine. Bring a saucepan of water to the boil and reduce the heat to simmer. Place the bowl over the simmering water and stir with a wooden spoon for about 5–10 minutes until the mixture thickens and lightly coats the back of the spoon. Remove from the heat and allow to cool. Stir in the bourbon.
2. Beat the cream and egg whites in separate bowls until soft peaks form. Fold the cream, then the egg whites into the bourbon mixture in two batches. Pour into glasses and sprinkle with grated nutmeg.

Cardamom, Orange and Plum Cakes

Serves 8

185 g (6 1/2 oz) unsalted butter, chopped
95 g (3 1/4 oz/1/2 cup) soft brown sugar
115 g (4 oz/1/2 cup) caster (superfine) sugar
3 eggs
1 teaspoon finely grated orange zest
310 g (11 oz/2 1/2 cups) self-raising flour, sifted
1 teaspoon ground cardamom
185 ml (6 fl oz/3/4 cup) milk
4 tinned plums, drained and patted dry, cut in half
1 tablespoon raw (demerara) sugar
thick (double/heavy) cream, to serve

1. Preheat the oven to 180°C (350°F/Gas 4). Lightly grease eight 250 ml (9 fl oz/1 cup) ceramic ramekins and dust with flour, shaking out any excess flour.

2. Cream the butter and sugars in a bowl using electric beaters until pale and fluffy. Add the eggs, one at a time and beating well after each addition, then stir in the orange zest. Fold the flour and cardamom into the butter mixture alternately with the milk until combined and smooth.

3. Divide the mixture between the ramekins and place a plum half, cut side down, on top of the batter. Sprinkle with raw sugar, place the ramekins on a baking tray and bake for 30–35 minutes, or until golden and firm to the touch. Serve warm or at room temperature with thick cream.

Fruit Cake

Serves 6–8

FRUIT CAKE MIXTURE

500 g (1 lb 2 oz/4 cups) sultanas (golden raisins)

350 g (12 oz/2 cups) chopped raisins

250 g (9 oz/1 2/3 cups) currants

250 g (9 oz/1 cup) quartered glacé cherries

250 ml (9 fl oz/1 cup) brandy or dark rum

225 g (7 3/4 oz) butter

225 g (7 3/4 oz/2 1/4 cups) dark brown sugar

2 tablespoons apricot jam

2 tablespoons treacle or golden syrup

1 tablespoon grated orange or lemon zest

4 eggs

350 g (12 oz/2 3/4 cups) plain (all-purpose) flour, sifted

1 teaspoon ground ginger, sifted

1 teaspoon mixed (pumpkin pie) spice, sifted

1 teaspoon ground cinnamon, sifted

TOPPING

675 g (1 lb 8 oz/2 3/4 cups) chopped mixed glacé fruit, such as apricots, pineapple, ginger and cherries

1 tablespoon brandy or dark rum, to glaze

3 teaspoons powdered gelatine

1. To make the cake, put the sultanas, raisins, currants and glacé cherries in a bowl. Add the brandy and set aside to soak overnight.
2. Preheat the oven to 150°C (300°F/Gas 2). Grease a 23 cm (9 inch) round cake tin. Cut 2 strips of baking paper long enough to fit around

the outside of the tin and wide enough to come 5 cm (2 inches) above the top. Fold down a 2½ cm (1 inch) cuff along the top. Make diagonal cuts up to the fold line about 1 cm (½ inch) apart. Fit the strips around the inside of the tin, pressing the cuts so that they sit flat around the base. Cut 2 circles of baking paper, using the tin as a guide, and line the base. Wrap a folded piece of newspaper around the outside of the tin and tie securely with string.

3 Beat together the butter and sugar. Beat in the jam, treacle and citrus zest. Add the eggs, one at a time, beating after each addition.

4 Sift together the flour and spices and stir into the mixture alternately with the soaked dried fruit.

5 Spoon the mixture into the prepared tin. Tap the tin on a work surface to remove any air bubbles. Level the surface with a dampened hand. Sit the cake tin on several sheets of newspaper in the oven and bake for 3 hours. The newspaper will prevent the cake from burning on the outside and is quite safe as the oven is at a low temperature.

6 Brush with the remaining brandy and arrange the glacé fruit on top. Bake for a further 30 minutes, then cover with greased foil. Bake for 1 further hour, or until a skewer comes out clean when inserted into the centre of the cake.

7 In a bowl, sprinkle the gelatine over 2 tablespoons of boiling water. Leave for 1 minute, until spongy, and stir briskly with a fork to dissolve. Brush the gelatine over the hot cake, cover with baking paper and wrap in a tea towel. Cool completely in the tin and turn out.

Choc-ginger Puddings

Makes 10

320 g (11 1/4 oz/2 1/2 cups) raisins, chopped
200 g (7 oz/1 1/3 cups) currants
110 g (3 3/4 oz/2/3 cup) pitted dates, chopped
75 g (2 1/2 oz/1/3 cup) glacé ginger, chopped
160 g (5 3/4 oz/1 1/3 cups) sultanas (golden raisins)
100 g (3 1/2 oz/1 1/3 cups) dried pears, chopped
100 g (3 1/2 oz/1/2 cup) dried apricots, chopped
175 g (6 oz/1 cup) dark chocolate chips
75 g (2 1/2 oz/1/2 cup) pistachio nuts, chopped
125 ml (4 fl oz/1/2 cup) brandy
250 g (9 oz) unsalted butter, frozen and grated
185 g (6 1/2 oz/1 cup) soft brown sugar
1 tablespoon golden (dark corn) syrup
80 ml (2 1/2 fl oz/1/3 cup) orange juice
1 teaspoon finely grated orange zest
80 ml (2 1/2 fl oz/1/3 cup) lemon juice
1 teaspoon finely grated lemon zest
4 eggs, lightly beaten
1 teaspoon bicarbonate of soda (baking soda)
185 g (6 1/2 oz/1 1/2 cups) plain (all-purpose) flour
60 g (2 1/4 oz/1/2 cup) self-raising flour
2 teaspoons mixed (pumpkin pie) spice
2 teaspoons ground cinnamon
1 teaspoon ground nutmeg
80 g (2 3/4 oz/1 cup) fresh breadcrumbs
custard (see page 158), to serve

1. Put all the fruit, the chocolate and pistachio nuts into a large bowl and stir in the brandy. Cover with plastic wrap and leave overnight.
2. Bring 2 large saucepans of water to the boil. Cut a piece of calico into ten 30 cm (12 inch) squares. Put the calico in one of the saucepans of boiling water for 15 minutes, then remove with tongs and, with gloved hands, wring out the water.
3. Put the butter in a large bowl and stir in the sugar, golden syrup, zests, juices and the eggs. Add the combined sifted bicarbonate of soda, flours and spices in two batches. Stir in the fruit and the breadcrumbs.
4. Place a calico square on a flat surface and rub liberally with plain flour, leaving a border of calico around each edge. Place a loosely packed cup of the mixture into the centre of the cloth. Gather and tie the cloth into a neat ball, pleating the calico. Tie firmly with string around the top and tie the end of the string in a loop to enable you to lower the puddings into a saucepan using a wooden spoon. Repeat with all the mixture and calico.
5. Place half the puddings in each saucepan of boiling water, then sit the lids over the spoons to keep most of the steam in. Simmer for 1 hour. Hang overnight in a cool place to dry, then refrigerate in an airtight container. Keep for up to 1 month.
6. To reheat, lower the puddings into a pan of boiling water and boil for 30 minutes. Remove the cloths and serve individually, with custard.

Brandy Alexander Punch

Serves 16

750 ml (26 fl oz/3 cups) brandy
375 ml (13 fl oz/1 1/2 cups) crème de cacao
1.8 litres (63 fl oz/7 cups) cream (whipping)
ice cubes, to serve
freshly grated nutmeg, to dust
16 strawberries, halved, to garnish

1 Pour the brandy, crème de cacao and cream into a large bowl. Whisk to just combine. Add ice cubes to a 3.5 litres (120 fl oz/14 cups) punch bowl and pour in the brandy mixture. Sprinkle with grated nutmeg, then serve in cocktail glasses garnished with strawberry halves.

Icy Mint Julep

Serves 4–6

3 very large handfuls mint leaves, chopped
2 tablespoons sugar
1 tablespoon lemon juice
500 ml (17 fl oz/2 cups) pineapple juice
250 ml (9 fl oz/1 cup) boiling water
500 ml (17 fl oz/2 cups) ginger ale, chilled
mint leaves, to garnish

1. Put the mint leaves in a bowl and bruise with a wooden spoon to release the oils. Transfer to a heatproof jug and add the sugar, lemon juice, pineapple juice and boiling water. Mix, cover with plastic wrap and set aside for 30 minutes. Strain the liquid, then cover and refrigerate until well chilled.
2. Mix in the chilled ginger ale. Put ice cubes in glasses and pour in the drink. Garnish each glass with a few fresh mint leaves.

Chocolate Hazelnut Torte

Serves 10

500 g (1 lb 2 oz/3 1/3 cups) chopped dark chocolate
6 eggs
2 tablespoons Frangelico
165 g (5 3/4 oz/1 1/2 cups) ground hazelnuts
250 ml (9 fl oz/1 cup) cream (whipping)

CHOCOLATE TOPPING
200 g (7 oz/1 1/3 cups) chopped dark chocolate
185 ml (6 fl oz/3/4 cup) cream (whipping)
1 tablespoon Frangelico
12 whole hazelnuts, lightly roasted

1. Preheat the oven to 150°C (300°F/Gas 2). Grease a deep 20 cm (8 inch) round cake tin and line with baking paper.
2. Put the chocolate in a heatproof bowl. Half fill a saucepan with water and bring to the boil. Remove from the heat and place the bowl over the pan, making sure it is not touching the water. Stir occasionally until the chocolate is melted.
3. Put the eggs in a large heatproof bowl and add the Frangelico. Place the bowl over a saucepan of barely simmering water over low heat, making sure it does not touch the water. Beat the mixture until it is light and foamy. Remove from the heat.
4. Using a metal spoon, quickly fold the melted chocolate and ground nuts into the egg mixture until just combined. Whip the cream, fold into the mixture and pour into the tin. Place the tin in a shallow baking dish. Pour in enough hot water to come halfway up the side of the tin.

5. Bake for 1 hour, or until just set. Remove the tin from the baking dish. Cool to room temperature, cover with plastic wrap and refrigerate overnight.
6. Cut a 17 cm (7 inch) circle from heavy cardboard. Invert the chilled cake onto the disc so that the base of the cake becomes the top. Place on a wire rack over a baking tray and remove the baking paper. Allow the cake to return to room temperature before you start to decorate.
7. To make the topping, combine the chopped chocolate, cream and Frangelico in a small pan. Heat gently over low heat, stirring, until the chocolate is melted and the mixture is smooth.
8. Pour the chocolate mixture over the cake in the centre, tilting slightly to cover the cake evenly. Tap the baking tray gently on the bench so that the top is level and the icing runs completely down the side of the cake. Place the hazelnuts around the edge of the cake. Refrigerate just until the topping has set and the cake is firm. Carefully transfer the cake to a serving plate, and cut into thin wedges to serve.

Fresh Fruit Pavlova

Serves 6–8

6 egg whites
500 g (1 lb 2 oz/2 cups) caster (superfine) sugar
1 1/2 tablespoons cornflour (cornstarch)
1 1/2 teaspoons vinegar
500 ml (17 fl oz/2 cups) cream (whipping)
2 bananas, sliced
500 g (1 lb 2 oz/3 1/3 cups) strawberries, sliced
4 kiwi fruit, sliced
4 passionfruit, pulped

1. Preheat the oven to 150°C (300°F/Gas 2). Line a large baking tray with baking paper and draw a 26 cm (10 1/2 inch) circle on the paper. Turn the paper over and place on the tray. Beat the egg whites in a large dry bowl until soft peaks form. Gradually add all but 2 tablespoons of the sugar, beating well after each addition. Combine the cornflour and vinegar with the last of the sugar and beat for 1 minute before adding it to the bowl. Beat for 5–10 minutes, or until all the sugar has completely dissolved and the meringue is stiff and glossy. Spread onto the paper inside the circle.

2. Shape the meringue evenly, running the flat side of a palette knife along the edge and over the top. Run the palette knife up the edge of the meringue mixture all the way round, making furrows. This strengthens the pavlova and helps prevent the edge from crumbling, as well as being decorative.

3 Bake for 40 minutes, or until pale and crisp. Reduce the heat to 120°C (235°F/Gas 1/2) and bake for 15 minutes. Turn off the oven and cool the pavlova in the oven, using a wooden spoon to keep the door slightly ajar. When completely cooled, top with whipped cream and fruit. Drizzle with passionfruit pulp and serve.

Fruit Mince Pies

Makes 12

MINCEMEAT

275 g (9 3/4 oz/2 1/4 cups) raisins

150 g (5 1/2 oz/1 1/4 cups) sultanas (golden raisins), chopped

50 g (1 3/4 oz/1/3 cup) dried apricots, chopped

2 tablespoons chopped almonds

75 g (2 1/2 oz/1/3 cup) mixed peel

75 g (2 1/2 oz/1/3 cup) currants

1 apple, peeled and grated

1 teaspoon finely grated lemon zest

1 teaspoon finely grated orange zest

1 tablespoon lemon juice

225 g (8 oz/1 1/4 cups) soft brown sugar

1 teaspoon mixed (pumpkin pie) spice

1/4 teaspoon ground nutmeg

4 tablespoons brandy

50 g (1 3/4 oz) butter, melted

MINCE PIES

225 g (8 oz/1 3/4 cups) plain (all-purpose) flour

185 g (6 1/2 oz) butter, chilled and cubed

2 tablespoons caster (superfine) sugar

1 teaspoon custard powder

2 egg yolks

150 g (5 1/2 oz) mincemeat (see recipe above)

1. Place all the mincemeat ingredients together in a large bowl. Mix well with a wooden spoon. Spoon the mixture into airtight containers or sterilized jars and seal. Keep in a cool dark place for up to 3 months.
2. Place the flour, butter, sugar and custard powder in a food processor. Combine until fine and crumbly. Add the egg yolks and a little water and process until the mixture comes together. Turn out onto a lightly floured surface. Gently knead the pastry until smooth. Cover and chill for 15 minutes.
3. Preheat the oven to 180°C (350°F/Gas 4). Roll out the pastry between two sheets of baking paper until it is about 3 mm (1/8 inch) thick. Cut into circles using a 7 cm (2 3/4 inch) round pastry cutter. Ease the dough circles into greased shallow patty tins. Spoon in 1–2 teaspoons of the mincemeat filling. Re-roll the pastry trimmings. Cut into shapes and use to decorate the top of the mince pies. Bake for 10–15 minutes, or until golden.
4. Remove from the oven and transfer to a wire rack to cool. Serve either warm or cold. Store any leftover mincemeat.

Traditionally, mincemeat is made with suet, which is an animal fat. Butter is used in this recipe. Shredded suet is widely available from supermarkets. Mincemeat made with suet will keep for several years if it is stored in a dry, dark place in a screwtop jar.

Creamy Coconut Ice

Makes 30 pieces

250 g (9 oz/2 cups) icing (confectioners') sugar
1/4 teaspoon cream of tartar
400 g (14 oz/1 1/4 cups) tin condensed milk
315 g (11 oz/3 1/2 cups) desiccated coconut
2–3 drops pink food colouring

1. Grease a 20 cm (8 inch) square cake tin and line the base with baking paper.
2. Sift the icing sugar and cream of tartar into a bowl. Make a well and add the condensed milk. Using a wooden spoon, stir in half the coconut, then the remaining coconut. Mix well with your hands. Divide the mixture in half and tint one half pink. Using your hands, knead the colour through evenly.
3. Press the pink mixture evenly over the base of the tin, cover with the white mixture and press down firmly. Refrigerate for 1–2 hours, or until firm. Remove from the tin, remove the paper and cut into pieces. Store in an airtight container in a cool place for up to 3 weeks.

Strawberry Margarita

Serves 2

2 egg whites, lightly beaten
salt, to dust
12 ice cubes
60 ml (2 fl oz/1/4 cup) tequila
60 ml (2 fl oz/1/4 cup) strawberry liqueur
60 ml (2 fl oz/1/4 cup) lime juice cordial
60 ml (2 fl oz/1/4 cup) lemon juice
30 ml (1 fl oz) Cointreau

1 Frost the rim of a martini glass by dipping the rim of the glass into the frothy egg white, then in salt. Put the ice cubes in a blender with the tequila, strawberry liqueur, lime juice cordial, lemon juice and Cointreau. Blend well, then pour into the martini glass, taking care to avoid touching the rim of the glass.

Italian Christmas Cake

Serves 18–20

440 g (15½ oz/1¼ cups) honey
60 ml (2 fl oz/¼ cup) red wine
235 g (8½ oz/1½ cups) blanched almonds, toasted and chopped
450 g (1 lb/2 cups) glacé fruit (choose a mixture of orange, pear, peach and red cherries), chopped into large chunks
410 g (14½ oz/3⅓ cups) plain (all-purpose) flour
115 g (4 oz/½ cup) caster (superfine) sugar
60 g (2¼ oz/½ cup) unsweetened cocoa powder
80 g (2¾ oz) dark chocolate, finely chopped
¼ teaspoon bicarbonate of soda (baking soda)
½ teaspoon ground cinnamon
½ teaspoon ground nutmeg
a large pinch of ground cloves
1 teaspoon finely grated orange zest
1 teaspoon finely grated lemon zest

TOPPING
200 g (7 oz) glacé orange slices
30 g (1 oz) red glacé cherries
115 g (4 oz/⅓ cup) warm honey

1. Preheat the oven to 170°C (325°F/Gas 3). Lightly grease a 23 cm (9 inch) round spring-form cake tin and line the base with baking paper. Dust the side of the tin with a little flour, shaking off any excess.
2. Combine the honey and red wine in a small saucepan and heat, stirring often, over low–medium heat for 2 minutes, or until the honey has just melted and the mixture is smooth.

3 Combine the almonds, glacé fruit, flour, sugar, cocoa powder, chocolate, bicarbonate of soda, spices and citrus zest in a large bowl and stir to combine well. Pour in the honey mixture, then, using a wooden spoon, stir until a firm dough forms; it may be necessary to use your hands.

4 Transfer the mixture into the prepared tin and smooth the top. Bake for 60 minutes, or until a skewer inserted into the centre of the cake comes out a little sticky. Using the skewer, pierce the cake all over, decorate with the orange slices and cherries and then spoon over the warm honey. Return the cake to the oven and bake for a further 10 minutes. Allow to cool.

5 Remove the cake from the tin, leave to cool completely, then wrap in plastic wrap and store for 1–2 days before using. Slice thinly to serve.

Florentines

Makes 24

30 g (1 oz/1/4 cup) plain (all-purpose) flour
2 tablespoons chopped walnuts
2 tablespoons chopped flaked almonds
2 tablespoons finely chopped glacé cherries
2 tablespoons finely chopped mixed peel
75 g (2 1/2 oz) unsalted butter, chilled and cubed
45 g (1 1/2 oz/1/4 cup) soft brown sugar
180 g (6 oz/1 1/4 cups) chopped dark chocolate

1. Preheat the oven to 180°C (350°F/Gas 4). Line a baking tray with baking paper.
2. Sift the flour into a bowl. Add the walnuts, almonds, cherries and mixed peel. Stir, then make a well in the centre.
3. Combine the butter and sugar in a small saucepan and stir over low heat until the butter has melted and the sugar has dissolved. Remove from the heat and add to the dry ingredients.
4. Stir with a wooden spoon until just combined, being careful not to overbeat. Measure teaspoons of mixture at a time onto the tray, pushing off the spoon with a palette knife, and spreading with the palette knife. Leave about 7 cm (2 3/4 inches) between each one as they will spread. Press into neat 5 cm (2 inch) rounds. Bake for 5–7 minutes. Remove from the oven and while still soft, use a flat-bladed knife to push the biscuits into neat rounds. Cool on the tray for 5 minutes before transferring to a wire rack to cool thoroughly.

5 Put the chocolate in a heatproof bowl. Bring a saucepan of water to the boil, then remove from the heat. Sit the bowl over the saucepan, making sure the bowl does not touch the water. Stir until the chocolate has melted. Carefully spread with a flat-bladed knife on the underside of the florentines. Make a swirl pattern on the tops with a fork if you wish. Place the biscuits chocolate-side up on a wire rack, to set.

Florentines can be made several days before required and stored in an airtight container. You can use white chocolate instead of dark chocolate.

Glacé Fruit and Nut Loaf

Serves 12

50 g ($1\frac{3}{4}$ oz) unsalted butter, softened
55 g (2 oz/$\frac{1}{3}$ cup) soft brown sugar
2 tablespoons orange marmalade
2 eggs
125 g ($4\frac{1}{2}$ oz/1 cup) plain (all-purpose) flour
1 teaspoon baking powder
1 teaspoon ground nutmeg
200 g (7 oz/1 cup) chopped, pitted dried dates
240 g ($8\frac{1}{2}$ oz/$1\frac{1}{4}$ cups) chopped raisins
155 g ($5\frac{1}{2}$ oz/1 cup) brazil nuts
140 g (5 oz/$\frac{2}{3}$ cup) red, yellow and green glacé cherries, quartered
120 g ($4\frac{1}{4}$ oz/$\frac{1}{2}$ cup) chopped glacé pears or pineapple
120 g ($4\frac{1}{4}$ oz/$\frac{1}{2}$ cup) chopped glacé apricots
120 g ($4\frac{1}{4}$ oz/$\frac{1}{2}$ cup) chopped glacé peaches
120 g ($4\frac{1}{4}$ oz/$\frac{1}{2}$ cup) chopped glacé figs
100 g ($3\frac{1}{2}$ oz/1 cup) walnut halves
100 g ($3\frac{1}{2}$ oz/$\frac{2}{3}$ cup) blanched almonds

TOPPING
2 teaspoons powdered gelatine
2 tablespoons marmalade
150 g ($5\frac{1}{2}$ oz/$\frac{2}{3}$ cup) glacé pineapple or pear rings
100 g ($3\frac{1}{2}$ oz/$\frac{1}{2}$ cup) red, yellow and green glacé cherries
40 g ($1\frac{1}{2}$ oz/$\frac{1}{4}$ cup) blanched almonds, toasted

1. Preheat the oven to 150°C (300°F/Gas 2). Grease a deep 20 x 8 cm (8 x 3 1/4 inch) loaf (bar) tin and line the base and sides with baking paper.
2. Beat the butter, sugar and marmalade together until pale and creamy. Add the eggs and beat until combined.
3. Sift the flour, baking powder and nutmeg into a large bowl. Add the fruit and nuts and mix until each piece is coated in the flour. Stir into the egg mixture.
4. Put the mixture in the tin, pushing well into each corner. Bake for 1 1/2–1 3/4 hours, or until a skewer inserted into the centre comes out clean. Cool in the tin for 10 minutes before turning out. Remove the baking paper and transfer to a wire rack to cool.
5. To make the topping, sprinkle the gelatine over 2 tablespoons water and the marmalade in a small bowl. Bring a pan of water to the boil, then remove from the heat. Stand the bowl in the pan and stir until the gelatine has dissolved. Brush the top of the cake with some of the gelatine mixture, top with arranged pineapple, cherries and almonds. Brush or drizzle with more gelatine mixture and allow to set.

Rocky Road

Makes about 30 pieces

250 g (9 oz/$2\frac{3}{4}$ cups) pink and white marshmallows, halved
160 g ($5\frac{3}{4}$ oz/1 cup) unsalted peanuts, roughly chopped
105 g ($3\frac{1}{2}$ oz/$\frac{1}{2}$ cup) glacé cherries, halved
60 g ($2\frac{1}{4}$ oz/1 cup) shredded coconut
350 g (12 oz/$2\frac{1}{3}$ cups) chopped dark chocolate

1. Line the base and two opposite sides of a shallow 20 cm (8 inch) square cake tin with foil.
2. Put the marshmallows, peanuts, cherries and coconut into a large bowl and mix until well combined.
3. Put the chocolate in a heatproof bowl. Half fill a saucepan with water and bring to the boil. Remove from the heat and place the bowl over the pan, making sure it is not touching the water. Stir occasionally until the chocolate is melted.
4. Add the chocolate to the marshmallow mixture and toss until well combined. Spoon into the cake tin and press evenly over the base. Refrigerate for several hours, or until set. Carefully lift out of the tin, then peel away the foil and cut the rocky road into small pieces. Store in an airtight container in the refrigerator.

Buttered Rum Mugs

Serves 4

1 tablespoon sugar
250 ml (9 fl oz/1 cup) rum
500 ml (17 fl oz/2 cups) boiling water
4 teaspoons unsalted butter, softened

1. Place the sugar, rum and boiling water in a heatproof jug. Stir to dissolve the sugar, then divide among 4 mugs. Stir 1 teaspoon of butter into each mug and serve.

Butterless Rum Fruit Cake

Serves 12–14

310 g (11 oz/2 1/2 cups) sultanas (golden raisins)
250 g (9 oz/2 cups) raisins
225 g (8 oz/1 1/2 cups) currants
185 ml (6 fl oz/3/4 cup) vegetable oil
125 ml (4 fl oz/1/2 cup) dark rum
125 ml (4 fl oz/1/2 cup) orange juice
230 g (8 1/2 oz/1 cup) soft brown sugar
2 tablespoons treacle or golden syrup
1/2 teaspoon bicarbonate of soda (baking soda)
1 tablespoon grated orange zest
4 eggs, lightly beaten
185 g (6 1/2 oz/1 1/2 cups) plain (all-purpose) flour
60 g (2 1/4 oz/1/2 cup) self-raising flour
1 tablespoon mixed (pumpkin pie) spice
40 g (1 1/2 oz/1/4 cup) blanched whole almonds
80 g (2 3/4 oz/1/4 cup) apricot jam, to glaze

1 Preheat the oven to 150°C (300°F/Gas 2). Lightly grease a 20 cm (8 inch) round cake tin. Cut a double layer of baking paper into a strip long enough to fit around the outside of the tin and tall enough to come 5 cm (2 inches) above the edge of the tin. Fold down a cuff about 2 cm (3/4 inch) deep along the top. Make cuts along the cuff to the fold line, about 1 cm (1/2 inch) apart. Fit the strip around the inside of the tin, with the cuts on the base, so they sit flat. Trace the tin base on a doubled piece of baking paper and cut. Sit the paper circles in the base of the tin.

2. Combine the dried fruit, oil, rum, orange juice, sugar and treacle in a large saucepan and stir over medium heat until the sugar has dissolved. Bring to the boil, reduce the heat and simmer, covered, over low heat for 10 minutes. Remove from the heat and stir in the bicarbonate of soda, then cool to room temperature. Stir in the zest, eggs, sifted flours and mixed spice.
3. Spread the mixture into the prepared tin and smooth the surface, then arrange the whole almonds over the top of the cake. Bake for 2 hours 15 minutes, or until a skewer inserted into the centre of the cake comes out clean (the skewer may be slightly sticky if inserted into fruit). Allow to cool in the tin.
4. Heat the jam in a saucepan over low heat for 3–4 minutes, or until runny. Brush the top of the cake with the jam.
5. When storing the cake, cover the top with baking paper and then foil to keep it moist. This fruit cake will keep, stored in an airtight container, in a cool place for up to 1 month, or up to 3 months in the freezer.

Ice Cream Christmas Pudding

Serves 10

50 g ($1^3/4$ oz/$^1/3$ cup) almonds, toasted, chopped
45 g ($1^1/2$ oz/$^1/4$ cup) mixed peel
80 g ($2^3/4$ oz/$^1/2$ cup) chopped raisins
80 g ($2^3/4$ oz/$^2/3$ cup) sultanas (golden raisins)
50 g ($1^3/4$ oz/$^1/3$ cup) currants
80 ml ($2^1/2$ fl oz/$^1/3$ cup) rum
1 litre (35 fl oz/4 cups) vanilla ice cream
105 g ($3^1/2$ oz/$^1/2$ cup) red and green glacé cherries, quartered
1 teaspoon mixed (pumpkin pie) spice
1 teaspoon ground cinnamon
$^1/2$ teaspoon ground nutmeg
1 litre (35 fl oz/4 cups) chocolate ice cream

1. Mix the almonds, peel, raisins, sultanas, currants and rum in a bowl, cover with plastic wrap and leave overnight. Chill a 2 litre (70 fl oz) pudding basin (mould) in the freezer overnight.
2. Soften the vanilla ice cream slightly and mix in the glacé cherries. Working quickly, press the ice cream around the inside of the chilled basin, spreading it evenly to cover the base and side of the basin. Return the basin to the freezer and leave overnight. Check the ice cream a couple of times and spread it evenly to the top.
3. The next day, mix the spices and chocolate ice cream with the fruit mixture. Spoon it into the centre of the pudding bowl and smooth the top. Freeze overnight, or until very firm. Turn the pudding out onto a chilled plate and decorate. Cut into wedges to serve.

Summer Berries in Champagne Jelly

Serves 8

1 litre (35 fl oz/4 cups) champagne or sparkling white wine
$1^{1}/_{2}$ tablespoons powdered gelatine
250 g (9 oz) sugar
4 strips lemon zest
4 strips orange zest
250 g (9 oz/$1^{2}/_{3}$ cups) strawberries, hulled
250 g (9 oz/$1^{2}/_{3}$ cups) blueberries

1. Pour half the champagne into a bowl and let the bubbles subside. Sprinkle the gelatine over the top in an even layer. Leave until the gelatine is spongy—do not stir. Pour the remaining champagne into a large saucepan, add the sugar and zests and heat gently, stirring constantly, until all the sugar has dissolved.
2. Remove the saucepan from the heat, add the gelatine mixture and stir until thoroughly dissolved. Leave to cool completely, then remove the zest.
3. Divide the berries among eight 125 ml (4 fl oz/$^{1}/_{2}$ cup) stemmed wine glasses and gently pour the jelly over them. Refrigerate until set. Remove from the refrigerator 15 minutes before serving.

Profiteroles with Dark Chocolate Sauce

Serves 4–6

60 g (2 1/4 oz) butter, chopped
90 g (3 1/4 oz/3/4 cup) plain (all-purpose) flour
3 eggs, lightly beaten
dark chocolate sauce (see page 157), to serve

WHITE CHOCOLATE FILLING
30 g (1 oz/1/4 cup) custard powder
1 tablespoon caster (superfine) sugar
375 ml (13 fl oz/1 1/2 cups) milk
150 g (5 1/2 oz/1 cup) white chocolate melts (buttons), chopped
1 tablespoon Grand Marnier

1. Preheat the oven to 210°C (415°F/Gas 6–7). Line a baking tray with baking paper. Put the butter and 185 ml (6 fl oz/3/4 cup) water in a saucepan. Bring to the boil, then remove from the heat. Add the flour all at once. Return to the heat and stir until the mixture forms a smooth ball. Set aside to cool slightly.
2. Transfer the mixture to a bowl and, while beating, gradually add the eggs a little at a time, beating well after each addition, to form a thick, smooth, glossy paste.
3. Spoon 2 heaped teaspoons of the mixture onto the tray at 5 cm (2 inch) intervals. Sprinkle lightly with water and bake for 12–15 minutes, or until the dough is puffed. Turn off the oven. Pierce a small hole in the base of each profiterole with the point of a knife and return the profiteroles to the oven. Leave them to dry in the oven for 5 minutes.

4 To make the white chocolate filling, combine the custard powder and sugar in a saucepan. Gradually add the milk, stirring until smooth, then continue to stir over low heat until the mixture boils and thickens. Remove from the heat and add the white chocolate and Grand Marnier. Stir until the chocolate is melted. Cover the surface with plastic wrap and allow to cool. Stir the custard until smooth, then spoon into a piping bag fitted with a 1 cm (1/2 inch) plain nozzle. Pipe the filling into each profiterole. Serve with the warmed dark chocolate sauce.

The profiteroles can be made a day ahead if desired, but only fill just before serving.

Brandied Apple Cider

Serves 4

2 apples
750 ml (26 fl oz/3 cups) alcoholic cider
250 ml (9 fl oz/1 cup) brandy or Calvados

1 Thinly slice the apples into discs, discarding the ends, but do not core. Put the apples in a large heavy-based saucepan and add the cider and brandy or Calvados. Heat the liquid until it is almost boiling, being careful to not boil. Serve in heatproof glasses, with a few apple slices in each glass.

Rum Truffles

Makes about 25

200 g (7 oz/1 1/3 cups) finely chopped dark cooking chocolate
60 ml (2 1/4 fl oz/1/4 cup) cream (whipping)
30 g (1 oz) butter
50 g (1 3/4 oz) chocolate cake, crumbled
2 teaspoons dark rum, brandy or whisky
95 g (3 1/4 oz/1/2 cup) chocolate sprinkles

1. Line a baking tray with foil. Put the chocolate in a heatproof bowl. Combine the cream and butter in a small pan and stir over low heat until the butter melts and the mixture is just boiling. Pour the hot cream mixture over the chocolate and stir until the chocolate melts and the mixture is smooth.
2. Stir in the cake crumbs and rum. Refrigerate for 20 minutes, stirring occasionally, or until firm enough to handle. Roll heaped teaspoons of the mixture into balls.
3. Spread the chocolate sprinkles on a sheet of greaseproof paper. Roll each truffle in the sprinkles until evenly coated, then place on the baking tray. Refrigerate for 30 minutes, or until firm. Serve in small paper patty cups, if desired. Truffles can also be rolled in dark cocoa powder, if preferred.

Sherry Trifle

Serves 8

85 g (3 oz/1/3 cup) strawberry jelly (gelatine dessert) crystals
300 g (10 1/2 oz) jam sponge roll
80 ml (2 1/2 fl oz/1/3 cup) sherry
825 g (1 lb 13 oz/4 cups) tin peaches, drained, sliced
30 g (1 oz/1/4 cup) custard powder
250 ml (9 fl oz/1 cup) milk
60 g (2 1/4 oz/1/4 cup) caster (superfine) sugar
2 teaspoons natural vanilla extract
250 ml (9 fl oz/1 cup) cream (whipping)
powdered drinking chocolate, to garnish
strawberries, optional, to garnish

1. Make the jelly according to the directions on the packet and refrigerate until the mixture reaches the consistency of unbeaten egg white. Meanwhile, cut the sponge roll into 1 cm (1/2 inch) slices and arrange, leaving no gaps, around the side and base of a 2.5 litre (88 fl oz) glass bowl. Drizzle sherry evenly all over the sponge pieces.
2. Pour the jelly over the cake and refrigerate until set. When set, top with the peach slices and refrigerate.
3. Blend the custard powder with 125 ml (4 fl oz/1/2 cup) of the milk in a saucepan until smooth. Add the remaining milk, sugar and vanilla to the saucepan. Stir over medium heat for 5 minutes, or until the mixture boils and thickens, then pour into a large bowl and allow to cool, stirring often to prevent a skin forming. When cold but not completely set, pour and spread the custard evenly over the peaches. Refrigerate until cold.

4 Beat the cream in a large bowl until soft peaks form. Spread the whipped cream over the custard, forming peaks, then sprinkle with a little drinking chocolate. Decorate with strawberries if desired.

You can change the flavour of the jelly and the type of fruit according to your taste.

Spiced Treacle Gingerbreads

Makes about 36

140 g (5 oz) unsalted butter, softened
115 g (4 oz/2/3 cup) dark brown sugar
90 g (3 1/4 oz/1/4 cup) treacle or golden (dark corn) syrup
1 egg
250 g (9 oz/2 cups) plain (all-purpose) flour
30 g (1 oz/1/4 cup) self-raising flour
3 teaspoons ground ginger
2 teaspoons ground cinnamon
3/4 teaspoon ground cloves
3/4 teaspoon ground nutmeg
1 teaspoon bicarbonate of soda (baking soda)

ICING
1 egg white
1/2 teaspoon lemon juice
125 g (4 1/2 oz/1 cup) icing (confectioners') sugar, sifted
assorted food colourings

1 Lightly grease two baking trays. Beat the butter and sugar in a bowl with electric beaters until light and creamy, then beat in the treacle and egg. Fold in the combined sifted flours, spices and bicarbonate of soda. Turn out onto a lightly floured surface and knead for 2–3 minutes, or until smooth. Cover with plastic wrap and chill for 10 minutes.

2 Divide the dough in half and roll out between two sheets of baking paper to 5 mm (1/4 inch) thick. Lay the dough on the trays and chill for 15 minutes until just firm. Preheat the oven to 180°C (350°F/Gas 4).

3 Cut out the dough using a 7 cm (2 3/4 inch) heart-shaped cutter (or whatever shapes you prefer). Using a sharp knife, cut out a 1 cm (1/2 inch) hole at the top of each shape (you can thread ribbon through these holes to hang up the biscuits). Place on the trays and bake for 10 minutes. Remove from the oven and leave on the trays for 5 minutes before transferring to a wire cake rack to cool. When the biscuits are cold, decorate with the icing.

4 To make the icing, whisk the egg white until foamy. Add the lemon juice and sugar and stir until glossy. Tint the icing any colour you want, then spoon into paper piping bags or a small plastic bag, seal the end and snip off the tip. When decorated, leave the icing to set.

White Christmas

Makes 24

45 g ($1\frac{1}{2}$ oz/$1\frac{1}{2}$ cups) puffed rice cereal
100 g ($3\frac{1}{2}$ oz/1 cup) milk powder
125 g ($4\frac{1}{2}$ oz/1 cup) icing (confectioners') sugar
90 g ($3\frac{1}{4}$ oz/1 cup) desiccated coconut
80 g ($2\frac{3}{4}$ oz/$\frac{1}{3}$ cup) chopped red glacé cherries
80 g ($2\frac{3}{4}$ oz/$\frac{1}{3}$ cup) chopped green glacé cherries
55 g (2 oz/$\frac{1}{2}$ cup) sultanas (golden raisins)
250 g (9 oz) Copha (white vegetable shortening)

1. Line a shallow 28 x 18 cm ($11\frac{1}{4}$ x 7 inch) loaf (bar) tin with foil. Put the puffed rice, milk powder, icing sugar, coconut, glacé cherries and sultanas in a large bowl and stir. Make a well in the centre.
2. Melt the Copha over low heat, cool slightly, then add to the well in the puffed rice mixture. Stir with a wooden spoon until all the ingredients are moistened.
3. Spoon the mixture into the tin and smooth down the surface. Refrigerate for 30 minutes, or until completely set. Remove from the tin and discard the foil. Cut into small triangles to serve.

Cranberry and Vodka Sparkle

Serves 2

250 ml (9 fl oz/1 cup) cranberry juice, chilled
250 ml (9 fl oz/1 cup) lemonade or mineral water
4 teaspoons lime juice
60 ml (2 fl oz/1/4 cup) vodka
ice cubes, to serve

1 Combine the cranberry juice and lemonade or mineral water in a jug with the lime juice, vodka and a few ice cubes. Mix well, pour into two tall glasses and serve immediately.

Yule Log

Serves 8

60 g ($2\frac{1}{4}$ oz/$\frac{1}{2}$ cup) plain (all-purpose) flour
2 tablespoons unsweetened cocoa powder
3 eggs
90 g ($3\frac{1}{4}$ oz/$\frac{1}{3}$ cup) caster (superfine) sugar
50 g ($1\frac{3}{4}$ oz) unsalted butter, melted and cooled
1 tablespoon caster (superfine) sugar, extra

FILLING
150 g ($5\frac{1}{2}$ oz/1 cup) chopped white chocolate
125 ml (4 fl oz/$\frac{1}{2}$ cup) cream (whipping)
50 g ($1\frac{3}{4}$ oz/$\frac{1}{3}$ cup) hazelnuts, toasted and finely chopped

TOPPING
150 g ($5\frac{1}{2}$ oz/1 cup) chopped dark chocolate
125 ml (4 fl oz/$\frac{1}{2}$ cup) cream (whipping), extra
icing (confectioners') sugar, to dust

1. Preheat the oven to 180°C (350°F/Gas 4). Brush a 30 x 35 cm (12 x 14 inch) jam roll tin with oil or melted butter and line the base and sides with baking paper. Sift the flour and cocoa powder together twice. Cream the eggs and sugar until light and fluffy and increased in volume.

2. Sift the flour over the eggs and pour the butter around the edge of the bowl. Using a large metal spoon, gently fold the mixture together to combine the flour and butter. Take care not to overmix and lose too much volume.

3 Spread the mixture into the tin and bake for 12 minutes, or until the sponge springs back when lightly touched with your fingertips. Sprinkle the extra caster sugar over a clean tea towel. Turn the sponge out onto the tea towel close to one end. Roll the sponge and tea towel together lengthways and leave to cool.

4 To make the filling, put the white chocolate in a small heatproof bowl. Bring a small pan of water to the boil, then remove from the heat. Add the cream to the chocolate and stand the bowl over the pan of water, making sure the base of the bowl does not touch the water, until the chocolate is soft. Stir until smooth. Repeat with the dark chocolate and cream for the topping. Leave the white chocolate mixture until it has cooled to room temperature and is the consistency of cream. Leave the dark chocolate mixture until it cools to a spreadable consistency.

5 Beat the white chocolate mixture until soft peaks form—do not overbeat or the mixture will curdle. Unroll the sponge, remove the tea towel and spread with the filling, finishing 2 cm (3/4 inch) from the end. Sprinkle with the hazelnuts. Re-roll the sponge and trim the ends. Cut off one end on the diagonal and place it alongside the log to create a branch.

6 Place the yule log on a serving plate and spread the dark chocolate topping all over it. Run the tines of a fork along the length of the roll to give a 'bark' effect. Just before serving, dust with icing sugar. Decorate with some fresh green leaves.

Sago Plum Pudding

Serves 6–8

65 g ($2^1/_4$ oz/$^1/_3$ cup) sago
250 ml (9 fl oz/1 cup) milk
1 teaspoon bicarbonate of soda (baking soda)
140 g (5 oz/$^3/_4$ cup) dark brown sugar
160 g ($5^3/_4$ oz/2 cups) fresh breadcrumbs
80 g ($2^3/_4$ oz/$^2/_3$ cup) sultanas (golden raisins)
75 g ($2^1/_2$ oz/$^1/_2$ cup) currants
80 g ($2^3/_4$ oz/$^1/_2$ cup) dried dates, chopped
2 eggs, lightly beaten
60 g ($2^1/_4$ oz) unsalted butter, melted and cooled
raspberries, for decoration
blueberries, for decoration
icing (confectioners') sugar, for decoration
brandy butter (see page 156), chilled, to serve

1. Combine the sago and the milk in a small bowl. Cover the mixture and refrigerate overnight.

2. Prepare a large saucepan which will hold a 1.5 litre (52 fl oz) pudding basin (mould). Place the basin on a trivet in the saucepan and pour water into the saucepan to come halfway up the side of the basin. Remove the basin and grease it with melted butter and line the base with baking paper.

3. Transfer the soaked sago and milk to a large bowl and stir in the bicarbonate of soda until dissolved. Stir in the sugar, breadcrumbs, dried fruit, beaten eggs and melted butter and mix well. Spoon into the prepared basin and smooth the surface with wet hands.

4 Put the saucepan of water on to boil. To cover the pudding, place a sheet of foil on the bench, top with a piece of baking paper the same size and brush the paper with melted butter. Fold a pleat across the centre of the foil and paper to allow for expansion. Place the paper and foil, foil-side-up, over the basin (don't press it onto the pudding) and smooth it down the side of the basin. Tie a double length of string firmly around the basin, just under the rim, then tie another length of string around the first string to make a handle to lower the pudding into the water. The paper/foil lid prevents any moisture getting into the pudding and making it soggy.

5 Carefully lower the pudding into the saucepan and reduce the heat until the water is simmering quickly. Cover the saucepan and steam the pudding for 3½–4 hours, replenishing with boiling water when necessary. Carefully remove the pudding basin from the saucepan and test with a skewer. If it is not cooked, re-cover and cook until done.

6 Remove the coverings and leave for 5 minutes before turning the pudding out onto a large serving plate. Loosen the edges with a palette knife if necessary. Serve hot decorated with raspberries and blueberries and lightly dusted with icing sugar. Serve with brandy butter.

Shortbread

Makes 8 wedges

250 g (9 oz) butter
50 g (1 3/4 oz/1/2 cup) icing (confectioners') sugar
300 g (10 1/2 oz/2 1/2 cups) plain (all-purpose) flour
4 tablespoons rice flour

1. Preheat the oven to 140°C (275°F/Gas 1). Grease a baking tray. Beat together the butter and icing sugar until light and fluffy. Sift in the flours and combine well with a wooden spoon. Shape the dough into a ball and knead lightly until smooth. Pat the dough into a 23 cm (9 inch) circle, about 1 cm (1/2 inch) thick, on the prepared baking tray.
2. Pinch a decorative edge to the shortbread circle, using lightly floured fingers.
3. Score the top of the circle into even wedges. Prick all over with a fork. Bake for 35–40 minutes, or until the shortbread is set and browned. Cool on the tray for 2–3 minutes. Transfer to a wire rack. When it is almost cool, cut through the score marks into neat pieces. Cool the shortbread completely.

Panforte

Makes 1 cake

65 g ($2\frac{1}{4}$ oz/$\frac{3}{4}$ cup) flaked almonds
65 g ($2\frac{1}{4}$ oz/$\frac{1}{2}$ cup) chopped macadamia nuts
65 g ($2\frac{1}{4}$ oz/$\frac{1}{2}$ cup) chopped walnuts
225 g (8 oz/$1\frac{1}{4}$ cups) mixed dried fruit
75 g ($2\frac{1}{2}$ oz/$\frac{2}{3}$ cup) plain (all-purpose) flour, sifted
2 tablespoons unsweetened cocoa powder, sifted
1 teaspoon ground cinnamon, sifted
50 g ($1\frac{3}{4}$ oz/$\frac{1}{3}$ cup) chopped dark chocolate
50 g ($1\frac{3}{4}$ oz) unsalted butter
100 g ($3\frac{1}{2}$ oz/$\frac{1}{2}$ cup) caster (superfine) sugar
4 tablespoons honey

1. Preheat the oven to 180°C (350°F/Gas 4). Grease a shallow 20 cm (8 inch) round cake tin. Line the base with baking paper. Mix together the nuts and dried fruit in a large bowl. Add the flour, cocoa and cinnamon and stir until thoroughly combined. Make a well in the centre.

2. Stir the chopped chocolate, butter, sugar and honey in a small heavy-based saucepan over low heat until melted and thoroughly combined. Remove the pan from the heat. Add the butter mixture to the well in the dry ingredients. Using a wooden spoon, gradually combine the dry ingredients, but do not overbeat.

3. Spoon the mixture into the prepared tin and smooth the surface. Bake for 50 minutes, or until the cake is firm to the touch in the centre. Allow the panforte to cool in the tin before turning out. Cut the cake into thin wedges to serve.

Chocolate Rum Mousse

Serves 4

250 g (9 oz/1 2/3 cups) chopped dark chocolate
3 eggs
60 g (2 1/4 oz/1/4 cup) caster (superfine) sugar
2 teaspoons dark rum
250 ml (9 fl oz/1 cup) cream (whipping), softly whipped

1. Put the chocolate in a heatproof bowl. Half fill a saucepan with water and bring to the boil. Remove from the heat and place the bowl over the pan, making sure it is not touching the water. Stir occasionally until the chocolate has melted. Set aside to cool.
2. Beat the eggs and sugar in a small bowl for 5 minutes, or until thick, pale and increased in volume.
3. Transfer the mixture to a large bowl. Using a metal spoon, fold in the melted chocolate with the rum, leave the mixture to cool, then fold in the whipped cream until just combined.
4. Spoon into four 250 ml (9 fl oz/1 cup) ramekins or dessert glasses. Refrigerate for 2 hours, or until set.

Summer Puddings

Serves 4–6

150 g (5 1/2 oz/1 1/4 cups) fresh blackcurrants
150 g (5 1/2 oz/1 1/4 cups) fresh redcurrants
150 g (5 1/2 oz/1 1/4 cups) raspberries
150 g (5 1/2 oz/1 1/4 cups) blackberries
200 g (7 oz/1 1/3 cups) strawberries, hulled and halved
caster (superfine) sugar, to taste
6–8 slices white bread, crusts removed

1. Put the berries, except the strawberries, in a large saucepan with 125 ml (4 fl oz/1/2 cup) water and heat gently until the berries begin to collapse. Add the strawberries and turn off the heat. Add sugar, to taste. Set aside to cool.

2. Line six 150 ml (5 fl oz) moulds or a 1 litre pudding basin (mould) with the bread. For the small moulds, use 1 slice of bread for each, cutting a circle to fit the bottom and strips to fit the sides. For the large mould, cut a large circle out of 1 slice for the bottom and cut the rest of the bread into fingers. Drain a little juice off the fruit mixture. Dip one side of each piece of bread in the juice before fitting it, juice-side-down, into the mould, leaving no gaps. Do not squeeze the bread or flatten it or it will not absorb the juices as well.

3. Fill the centre of the mould with the fruit and add a little juice. Cover the top with a layer of dipped bread, juice-side-up, and cover with plastic wrap. Put a plate which fits inside the dish on the plastic wrap, then weigh it down. If you are using smaller moulds, stack them on top of each other to weigh them down. Refrigerate overnight. Carefully turn out the pudding and serve.

Stollen

Makes 1

80 ml ($2\frac{1}{2}$ fl oz/$\frac{1}{3}$ cup) lukewarm milk
2 teaspoons sugar
2 teaspoons (7 g/$\frac{1}{4}$ oz) dried yeast
125 g ($4\frac{1}{2}$ oz) butter, softened
90 g ($3\frac{1}{4}$ oz/$\frac{1}{3}$ cup) caster (superfine) sugar
1 egg
2 teaspoons natural vanilla extract
$\frac{1}{2}$ teaspoon ground cinnamon
375 g (13 oz/3 cups) strong flour
80 g ($2\frac{3}{4}$ oz/$\frac{2}{3}$ cup) raisins
75 g ($2\frac{1}{2}$ oz/$\frac{1}{2}$ cup) currants
95 g ($3\frac{1}{4}$ oz/$\frac{1}{2}$ cup) mixed peel
60 g ($2\frac{1}{4}$ oz/$\frac{1}{2}$ cup) slivered almonds
30 g (1 oz) butter, melted
icing (confectioners') sugar, to dust

1 Put the milk, sugar and yeast with 80 ml ($2\frac{1}{2}$ fl oz/$\frac{1}{3}$ cup) warm water in a small bowl and mix well. Leave in a warm, draught-free place for 10 minutes, or until bubbles appear on the surface. The mixture should be frothy and slightly increased in volume. If your yeast doesn't foam it is dead, so you will have to discard it and start again.

2 Cream the butter and sugar until light and creamy, then beat in the egg and vanilla. Add the yeast, cinnamon and most of the flour and mix to a soft dough, adding more flour if necessary. Turn out onto a lightly floured surface and knead for 10 minutes, or until the dough is smooth and elastic. Place in a lightly oiled bowl, cover with plastic wrap and leave in a draught-free place for $1\frac{3}{4}$ hours or until doubled in volume.

3. Knock back the dough by punching it to expel the air. Press it out to a thickness of about 1.5 cm (5/8 inch). Sprinkle the fruit and nuts over the dough, then gather up and knead for a few minutes to mix the fruit and nuts evenly through the dough.
4. Shape the dough into an oval about 18 cm (7 inches) wide and 30 cm (12 inches) long. Fold in half lengthways, then press down to flatten slightly, with the fold slightly off centre on top of the loaf. Place on the tray, cover with plastic wrap and leave in a warm place for 1 hour, or until doubled in size. Preheat the oven to 180°C (350°F/Gas 4). Lightly grease a baking tray.
5. Bake the dough for 40 minutes, or until golden. As soon as it comes out of the oven, brush with the melted butter, allowing each brushing to be absorbed until you have used all the butter. Cool on a wire rack. Dust with icing sugar.

Stollen is a rich fruit bread from Germany that is now known internationally as a special Christmas treat. Sometimes a filling such as marzipan is put in the centre.

Hot Toddy

Serves 4

1 tablespoon soft brown sugar
4 lemon slices
4 cinnamon sticks
12 whole cloves
125 ml (4 fl oz/$^{1}/_{2}$ cup) whisky
1 litre (35 fl oz/4 cups) boiling water
sugar, to taste

1. Put the sugar, lemon, cinnamon, cloves, whisky and boiling water in a heatproof jug. Stir to combine and leave to infuse for a few minutes, then strain. Add more sugar, to taste. Serve in heatproof glasses.

Jam Puddings

Serves 6

185 g ($6^1/2$ oz) unsalted butter, softened
185 g ($6^1/2$ oz/$^3/4$ cup) caster (superfine) sugar
1 teaspoon natural vanilla extract
3 eggs, lightly beaten
60 g ($2^1/4$ oz/$^1/2$ cup) plain (all-purpose) flour
125 g ($4^1/2$ oz/1 cup) self-raising flour
160 g ($5^1/2$ oz/$^1/2$ cup) berry jam
custard (see page 158), to serve

1. Preheat the oven to 180°C (350°F/Gas 4). Lightly grease six 250 ml (9 fl oz/1 cup) fluted or plain heatproof moulds.
2. Beat the butter, sugar and vanilla until light and creamy. Add the eggs gradually, beating well after each addition. Using a metal spoon, fold in the combined sifted flours, a quarter at a time.
3. Spoon the mixture evenly into the moulds and smooth the surface. Cover each with a piece of greased foil, pleated in the middle. Secure with string. Place in a large deep baking dish filled with enough boiling water to come halfway up the sides of the moulds. Bake for 45 minutes, or until a skewer comes out clean. Put the jam in a small pan and warm over low heat for 3–4 minutes, or until liquid. Leave the puddings for 5 minutes before loosening the sides with a knife and turning out. Top with the jam. Serve with custard or ice cream.

Glazed Berry Tart

Serves 4–6

125 g (4 1/2 oz/1 cup) plain (all-purpose) flour
90 g (3 1/4 oz) unsalted butter, chilled, cubed
2 tablespoons icing (confectioners') sugar
1–2 tablespoons iced water

FILLING
3 egg yolks
2 tablespoons caster (superfine) sugar
2 tablespoons cornflour (cornstarch)
250 ml (9 fl oz/1 cup) milk
1 teaspoon natural vanilla extract
250 g (9 oz/1 2/3 cups) strawberries, halved
125 g (4 1/2 oz/3/4 cup) blueberries
125 g (4 1/2 oz/1 cup) raspberries
150 g (5 1/2 oz/1/2 cup) redcurrant jelly

1. Preheat the oven to180°C (350°F/Gas 4). Lightly grease a 20 cm (8 inch) round, loose-based, fluted tart (flan) tin. Sift the flour into a bowl and rub in the butter, using your fingertips, until the mixture resembles fine breadcrumbs. Mix in the sugar. Make a well in the centre and add almost all the water. Mix with a flat-bladed knife, using a cutting action, until the mixture comes together in beads, adding more water if the dough is too dry.

2. Roll out the pastry between two sheets of baking paper to fit the base and side of the tart tin. Line the tin with the pastry and trim away any excess. Refrigerate for 20 minutes. Line the tin with baking paper and pour in baking beads or uncooked rice. Bake for 15 minutes,

then remove the paper and beads. Bake the pastry for another 15 minutes, or until golden.

3 To make the filling, place the egg yolks, sugar and cornflour in a bowl and whisk until pale. Heat the milk in a small saucepan until almost boiling, then remove from the heat and add gradually to the egg mixture, beating constantly. Strain into the saucepan. Stir constantly over low heat for 3 minutes, or until the mixture boils and thickens. Remove from the heat and add the vanilla. Transfer to a bowl, cover with plastic wrap and set aside to cool.

4 Spread the filling in the pastry shell and top with berries. Warm the redcurrant jelly in a small pan until it melts. Brush the jelly over the fruit with the pastry brush.

You can cook the pastry up to a day ahead and fill the tart up to 4 hours before serving.

Chocolate Hazelnut Drink

Serves 2

500 ml (17 fl oz/2 cups) milk
80 g (2¾ oz/¼ cup) chocolate hazelnut spread
50 g (1¾ oz/⅓ cup) finely chopped dark chocolate
cream (whipping), to serve
hazelnuts, chopped, toasted, to serve

1. Put the milk, hazelnut spread and dark chocolate in a saucepan and heat slowly, without boiling. Stir constantly for 5 minutes, or until the chocolate has melted. Divide the liquid between 2 mugs and top with the whipped cream and hazelnuts.

Mulled Wine

Serves 6

12 cloves

2 oranges

60 g (2 1/4 oz/1/4 cup) sugar

1 whole nutmeg, freshly grated

4 cinnamon sticks

2 lemons, thinly sliced

750 ml (26 fl oz/3 cups) full-bodied red wine

1. Push the cloves into the outside zest of the oranges and place in a saucepan with the sugar, nutmeg, cinnamon and lemon. Pour in 500 ml (17 fl oz/2 cups) water and bring to the boil, then reduce the heat, cover the pan and simmer for 20 minutes. Allow to cool, then strain and discard the fruit and spices.
2. Pour the mixture into a saucepan, add wine and heat until almost boiling—do not allow to boil or the alcohol will evaporate off. Serve in heatproof glasses.

Steamed Pudding

Serves 10–12

650 g (1 lb 7 oz/5 cups) mixed sultanas (golden raisins), currants and raisins
330 g ($11^1/_2$ oz/$1^3/_4$ cups) mixed dried fruit, chopped
45 g ($1^1/_2$ oz/$^1/_4$ cup) mixed peel
125 ml (4 fl oz/$^1/_2$ cup) brown ale
2 tablespoons brandy or rum
80 ml ($2^1/_2$ fl oz/$^1/_3$ cup) orange juice
80 ml ($2^1/_2$ fl oz/$^1/_3$ cup) lemon juice
1 teaspoon finely grated orange zest
1 teaspoon finely grated lemon zest
225 g (8 oz) suet, grated
245 g (9 oz/$1^1/_3$ cups) soft brown sugar
3 eggs, lightly beaten
200 g (7 oz/$2^1/_2$ cups) fresh breadcrumbs
90 g ($3^1/_4$ oz/$^2/_3$ cup) self-raising flour
1 teaspoon mixed (pumpkin pie) spice
$^1/_4$ teaspoon freshly grated nutmeg
100 g ($3^1/_2$ oz/$^2/_3$ cup) blanched almonds, roughly chopped
whisky sauce (see page 154), to serve

1. Put the sultanas, currants, raisins, mixed dried fruit, mixed peel, brown ale, rum, orange and lemon juices and zests into a large bowl and stir together. Cover and leave overnight.

2. Add the suet, brown sugar, eggs, breadcrumbs, flour, spices, almonds and a pinch of salt to the bowl and mix well. The mixture should fall from the spoon—if it is too stiff, add a little more ale.

3. Put a 2 litre (70 fl oz) pudding basin (mould) on a trivet or upturned saucer in a large saucepan with a lid, and pour in enough water to come halfway up the side of the basin. Remove the basin and grease it with melted butter and line the base with baking paper.

4. Spread the mixture into the prepared basin, smoothing the top to make it level. Put the saucepan of water on to boil. To cover the pudding, place a sheet of foil on the bench, top with a piece of baking paper the same size and brush the paper with melted butter. Fold a pleat across the centre of the foil and paper to allow for expansion. Place the paper and foil, foil-side-up, over the basin (don't press it onto the pudding) and smooth it down the side of the basin. Tie a double length of string firmly around the basin, just under the rim, then tie another length of string around the first string to make a handle to lower the pudding into the water. The paper/foil lid prevents any moisture getting into the pudding and making it soggy.

5. Carefully lower the pudding into the saucepan and reduce the heat until the water is simmering quickly. Cover the saucepan and steam the pudding for 8 hours, replenishing with boiling water when necessary. If you want to keep the pudding to serve later on, steam it for 6 hours now and for another 2 hours on the day you wish to eat it. Remove the pudding and test with a skewer. If it is not cooked, re-cover and cook until done. Stand the pudding for 5 minutes before turning onto a large plate. If the pudding sticks, ease down the sides with a palette knife. Serve the pudding hot, cut into wedges, with whisky sauce.

Individual Christmas Cakes

Makes 12

1 quantity fruit cake mixture (see page 164)

HOLLY LEAVES AND BERRIES
65 g (2 1/4 oz) marzipan
green and red food colouring
icing sugar

ROYAL ICING
1 egg white
250 g (9 oz/2 cups) icing (confectioners') sugar, sifted
2–3 teaspoons lemon juice

1. Preheat the oven to 150°C (300°F/Gas 2). Lightly grease 12 muffin tins and line the bases with a circle of baking paper. Fill to the top with the cake mixture and smooth the surface. Bake for 1 1/4 hours, or until a skewer inserted into the centre comes out clean. Cool in the tins before turning out to decorate, so the small base becomes the top.

2. To make the holly leaves, knead 50 g (1 3/4 oz) of marzipan until it is soft. Roll out as thinly as possible on a surface lightly dusted with icing sugar. Cut out the leaves with a cutter or template. Pinch the leaves in half, open out and press the edges gently to curl in different directions. Set aside to dry on a sheet of greaseproof paper. Brush green colouring around the edge of each leaf—don't put on too much colour or it will bleed.

3. Knead a little red colouring into the remaining marzipan and roll into small balls to make berries. Paint or roll the berries through the colouring to coat thoroughly. Dry on greaseproof paper.

4 To make the royal icing, lightly beat the egg white with a wooden spoon. Gradually add the icing sugar, beating to a smooth paste. Slowly add the lemon juice until slightly runny. Spread a tablespoon of icing over each cake, using a palette knife to smooth and letting some drizzle down the sides. Secure holly leaves on top and a few berries, using a little leftover icing.

These cakes can be stored in an airtight container in a single layer in a cool dark place for up to 1 month after icing.

index